MUSIC
Its Story in
the West

ALAN KENDALL

This edition produced exclusively for

 WHSMITH

For Pauline and Raymond Simkins

© Alan Kendall 1980

This edition produced exclusively for W. H. Smith by
George Weidenfeld and Nicolson Limited
91 Clapham High Street, London SW4

Designed by Norman Reynolds
Picture research by Claire Cockburn

ISBN 0 297 77876 5

Filmset by Keyspools Ltd, Golborne, Lancashire
Colour separations by Newsele Litho Ltd
Printed and bound in Italy by L.E.G.O., Vicenza

Contents

1 The Middle Ages and
Early Renaissance   9
2 The Renaissance   49
3 Baroque   79
4 The Classical Style   127
5 Romanticism   167
6 The Twentieth Century   203
List of Key Works   248
Glossary   250
Acknowledgments   252
Index   254

A hurdy-gurdy, from the
Paris Conservatoire
Collection, which once
belonged to Madame
Adélaïde (1732–1800), the
fourth daughter of Louis
XV of France.

Introduction

Today music is available to more people than ever before, and technical developments, together with continuing improvements in musical standards, mean that we have the opportunity to hear not only more acutely and more readily but also more faithfully what the composer originally intended. What in the past remained principally the domain of scholars is now communicated directly to the public. This in turn has stimulated interest in the composers themselves and the factors that influenced their lives and their works.

There are many people who, while they love music and could not imagine life without it, do not read it, and for whom the more technical aspects of it are meaningless. Nevertheless they are interested in how music came about, what gave rise to it, why it changed direction at certain moments, and how successive generations have reacted to it. This book is aimed at that audience. No specific musical extracts are used for discussion, and no technical terms are introduced without explanation.

In such a small compass one cannot hope to be exhaustive, and indeed endless lists of names and dates would simply confuse. The emphasis therefore lies as far as possible on isolating the main streams of development. Then again, to attempt to compress such a vast time-span into one book necessarily involves a certain amount of selectivity. Most attention has been given to the later Baroque, Classical and Romantic periods – what for most people constitutes 'classical' music – since the composers representative of those periods are the ones whose music is most often heard, and about whom the music-lover is most likely to want to know. Consideration is also given to medieval and Renaissance music, interest in which is increasing all the time, and, at the opposite end of the time-scale, to the more significant modern developments.

This book is therefore essentially a point of departure; it aims to provide a historical framework, at the same time to act as a stimulus for further exploration of the story of music in the West, and ideally to assist in the enjoyment of music itself.

A caricature by Grandville of Berlioz conducting a huge Romantic orchestra. The presence of the cannon suggests the effect on contemporary listeners of such a volume of sound.

7

I. The Middle Ages & Early Renaissance

An illustration by the Flemish artist who decorated the Isabella Breviary (*c.* 1479), now in the British Museum. Musicians line the steps to the Temple in Jerusalem. The section of Psalms from 120 to 134, known as the Gradual Psalms, was probably sung by pilgrims as they went up to Jerusalem.

The influence of the Church

In common with so much at the heart of our civilization, music in the West came to us through the Early Christian Church. In its use of music the Church was not only harnessing a very basic human instinct, but was also following the example of Christ and His disciples in their singing of the Passover Hymn before leaving the room in which the Last Supper was held. This incident, recorded in the gospels of Matthew (XXVI: 30) and Mark (XIV: 26), is a reminder of one very important strand in the development of the music of the Early Church – contemporary Jewish practice. The Jewish psalms, or Psalms of David as they are often known, were one of the most precious gifts that the Christian Church ever received; not only were they incorporated into the Bible as literature created by divine inspiration but they have been firmly embedded in the Christian liturgy ever since, and their particular verse form had a direct effect on the music that evolved for their performance.

As the Church spread westward, north into Asia Minor and Europe and south into Africa, it encountered and often assimilated local tendencies. For example, St Paul, writing to the Christians at Ephesus (Ephesians V: 19), exhorted them to 'speak to one another in psalms, hymns and spiritual songs: sing and make music in your hearts to the Lord', and earlier in the same chapter actually incorporated some words of a hymn into his text. Pliny the Younger, round about AD 112, wrote that the Christians in the province of Bithynia in Asia Minor were in the habit of singing (or perhaps reciting) 'a song to Christ as a god'. In fact the oldest surviving example of Christian music is part of a hymn in praise of the Trinity, contained in a papyrus found on the site of the Egyptian town of Oxyrhynchos, dating from the late third century. The words and notation, or method of writing down the musical notes, are Greek. Generally speaking, however, music developed very slowly in the first three centuries of the Church's history because it represented a persecuted minority; services had to be short and simple since they were usually held in secret. The Christians were persecuted by successive Roman emperors, especially Nero (37–68) and Domitian (reigned 81–96) in the first century AD, and Diocletian (reigned 284–305) in the third.

Under Diocletian's successor, Constantine the Great, the whole position of the Christian Church changed dramatically: in 313 the new Emperor granted toleration and freedom of worship. Now churches might be built, worship become public, and services be conducted with greater magnificence and ceremony. Naturally music came to play a part in them. Soon St Basil (*c.*330–79) was able to write: 'God blended the delight of melody with doctrines in order that through the pleasantness and softness of the sound we might unawares receive what was useful in words ... For this purpose these harmonious melodies of the Psalms have been designed for us.' Later we shall consider what exactly these 'harmonious melodies of the Psalms' were, but St Basil's confident assertion conceals a great dilemma for the Early Church. The Jewish religion has been mentioned as the first important strand in the development of the music of the Early Church; the second strand was the music of Ancient Greece.

Unfortunately precious little is known about Greek music itself. Two Delphic hymns to Apollo survive, dating from about 150 BC, a *skolion* or drinking song from the same period, or possibly later, and three hymns of Mesomedes of Crete which date from the second century AD. We have much more precise information about Greek musical terminology, theory of acoustics and scale formation, and we know that in general terms the music consisted of long strands of relatively simple melody closely allied with text, and that there was a strong tradition of improvization, though often incorporating various traditional Greek musical conventions. Finally, we know from the writings of Plato (*c.*427–347 BC) and Aristotle (384–322 BC) that a philosophy of music had developed that saw it not as an art form in the modern sense, but as a positive force in human affairs.

It was primarily this last aspect that the Early Church had to reckon with, for in Greece music had been a part of the games and rituals that were now considered pagan. Moreover as Rome took over Greek music, along with almost everything else, it became more debased and coarse, to the extent that it was largely thought of as an incitement to immorality. The longstanding reluctance to accept organs in churches was not an irrational prejudice on the part of the Church authorities, but mainly because the early organ, known as the *hydraulos*, was almost entirely identified with the cruel sports of the arena, and, being designed for the open air, was both huge and loud. Even if churches had been able to accommodate such organs, let alone afford them, there was still a very understandable emotional obstacle to be overcome – too many Christians had perished in those same arenas.

In its fight against paganism the Church had to make up its mind not just about the use of the organ but about all musical instruments

ABOVE The harp is one of the oldest and most widespread of musical instruments, as this clay plaque (*c.* 2000–1800 BC) from Mesopotamia shows. It is distinguished from the lyre in having its strings perpendicular to, and not parallel with, the sound board.

RIGHT The first of two paeans – hymns of praise or triumph – to Apollo, on the wall of the Treasury of the Athenians at Delphi in Greece (*c.* 138 BC). Scholars have succeeded in transcribing this Greek notation.

in connection with the ritual. Despite the fact that they were referred to in the Old Testament – David himself was a harpist – and were used in the Jewish liturgy, the far-reaching decision was taken that all instruments would be excluded, and so for virtually the first thousand years of its history Church music was destined to be unaccompanied. Luckily music was not banned entirely, for the consequences would have been difficult to imagine. Even then there was sufficient anxiety in the Church for St Augustine of Hippo (354–430) to stipulate that a true hymn must incorporate three elements: praise, praise of God, and these sung. Of course the problem did not arise with the Psalms, since the 'content' was never in doubt. The way in which the various elements in Church music were organized subsequently gave Western music its next great impetus.

The Mosaon amphora in the Staatliche Antikensammlung, Munich, shows two types of lyre: on the left is the *barbiton*, and next to it the larger *phorminx*. The dancing figure holds *krotala* or clappers, and the figure far right the double pipes known as an *aulos*.

The division of the Roman Empire into two parts meant effectively that, as far as the West was concerned, ecclesiastical authority was concentrated in Rome, while in the East it was vested in Byzantium or Constantinople until the collapse of the Byzantine Empire in 1453 – though the separation of the two Churches in fact took place in 1054. As we have seen, local traditions tended to vary, but with all the authority of Rome behind him Pope Gregory I (c.540–604) undertook to bring a standard form of liturgy and chant to the West, and with the notable exception of Ambrosian Chant in Milan he succeeded brilliantly. Some three thousand melodies were gathered together under his control, and it is these tunes that the Church still regards as the official ones today, and which are known collectively as Gregorian Chant, in his honour. This did not mean, of course, that in practice no new chants were composed. The Golden Age of the chant lasted from the fifth to the eighth centuries, and was followed by a Silver Age from the ninth to the twelfth centuries. During that period many more new tunes, as well as texts, were written.

By this time the Eucharist – a Greek word meaning 'thanksgiving' (but in fact a mystical re-enactment of Christ's actions during the course of the Last Supper, of which thanksgiving was part) – had become the heart of the dignified ceremony, observed with increasing ritual in words and music, known as the Mass. Today it is the chief service in both the Roman Catholic and the Anglican Church. Its form and concept have inspired musicians through the centuries, and continue to do so even now, despite the fact that the concept of Christendom as such has ceased to have any real meaning.

As well as the Mass itself there were services called the Canonical Hours or Offices, starting with Nocturns at midnight, Lauds at daybreak, and so on through Prime, Terce, Sext, None, Vespers and Compline. Nowadays only monastic communities tend to observe them, and indeed it was really the monastic movement that produced them. At the Reformation the Anglican Church took over Nocturns and Lauds as Matins or Morning Prayer, and Vespers and Compline as Evensong or Evening Prayer, which later became the principal morning and evening services of the new prayer book. We shall see in due course what implications this was to have for composers of religious music for the Reformed Churches.

Of course music existed outside the Church too in these early centuries. People sang and played as they went about their work or rested at home together, but unfortunately none of it is known to us; the people most likely to have recorded it, simply because they were educated, were men in holy orders, and such references as there are to secular music tend, on the whole, to be hostile. Nevertheless it is more than likely that some of the music heard outside ecclesiastical establishments found its way inside, and doubtless the system operated in the opposite direction, too, even if it was only musical snatches that were assimilated rather than complete phrases or whole tunes. As time went by it was inevitable that music should flourish in

Pope Gregory the Great from the Hartker Antiphoner (c.980–1011). The Pope is dictating to a scribe, and the dove, symbolizing the Holy Spirit, whispers what he is to say.

a secular as well as a religious context, and it is to secular music that we will turn next.

Secular music

It is extremely difficult to form any very precise idea of what secular music from the sixth to the tenth centuries actually sounded like. None has survived from earlier than the ninth century, and what we have from the ninth and tenth centuries is virtually impossible to read because of the problem of interpreting the system of notation. It is only through the work of Guido of Arezzo (c.995–1050) that we have

RIGHT In the eleventh century Guido of Arezzo introduced this mnemonic device, known as the Guidonian Hand, as an aid to singing at sight. The tips and joints of the fingers had notes allotted to them, and once the singer had learnt the placing of each note, he could then practise.

LEFT An illustration from the *Roman de Fauvel* (c. 1300) in the Bibliothèque Nationale, Paris. Fauvel was a horse or ass, whose name was derived from the first letters of the vices of *Flaterie, Avarice, Vilanie, Variété* (or *Vanité*), *Envie* and *Lascheté*. Anyone thought guilty of some or all of these vices was subjected to a serenade of extemporary music with pans, trays etc. known as a charivari.

any real information on the tunes of the eleventh century and later medieval period. Of course in one respect this is not at all surprising. Folk music was handed down orally from generation to generation, and no one capable of writing it down thought it necessary to do so. It was only through the determined efforts of some dedicated musicians in the nineteenth and early twentieth centuries that a great deal of Western folk music was written down – otherwise it would have disappeared forever in the face of increasing urbanization and the breakdown of traditional ways of life.

The lyrics of some of the songs have survived, however, with the occasional addition of tunes in an undeciphered notation known as staffless neumes. Most of the texts are in Latin, the language used in educated circles, but by the eleventh century songs began to be written down in the vernacular, or language of a particular area. Who performed these songs, and how did they organize themselves, bearing in mind the fact that they did not belong to any of the existing bodies of Church music? The secular musicians who flourished throughout the tenth and eleventh centuries can be put into two main groups. First were the men known as goliards, who were supposed to have taken their name from their patron, a bishop called Golias, though he seems to have been entirely fictitious. The goliards were mostly students, educated young men who had been taught in an ecclesiastical establishment but had not taken full priestly or monastic vows, and who roamed around Britain, France and Germany. Their songs are of the coming of spring, of love, drink, and their superiors – the last of these often bitterly satirical, which ultimately brought reprisals from the authorities. It is a pity that we cannot hear them with their original tunes, although Carl Orff's *Carmina Burana* (1936) sets some of the texts to music, and gives us something of their flavour.

The uneducated counterparts of the goliards were the jongleurs or gleemen. They differed from the goliards in a number of ways: as their French name suggests, there was a large element of the popular entertainer or juggler in their performance; they did not write their own songs; and they sang them in the vernacular. Such songs were known as *chansons de geste* and were often huge epic narratives, such as the *Chanson de Roland*. The jongleurs represented an older strain in popular entertainment than the goliards, and lasted much longer, for the goliards tended to be absorbed in the early thirteenth century when universities began to grow and scholars stayed in one place. The jongleurs, however, organized themselves into brotherhoods and guilds, and by the fourteenth century had become relatively respectable, partly as a result of their association with the refinement of the troubadours and *trouvères*. They were, no doubt unwittingly, witnessing the first great blossoming of secular musical art.

The art of the troubadours originated in the south of France, where the language spoken in the Middle Ages was Provençal, or *langue d'oc*. *Oc* was the Provençal word for 'yes', whereas in the north it was

Much early secular music was closely allied to performances by tumblers and jugglers, and the pipe and tabor provided the basis of dance music from the thirteenth century onwards. The pipe was in fact a duct flute, and the tabor a small drum with a gut snare to give an additional rattling or buzzing effect. This illustration is from a manuscript in the British Museum.

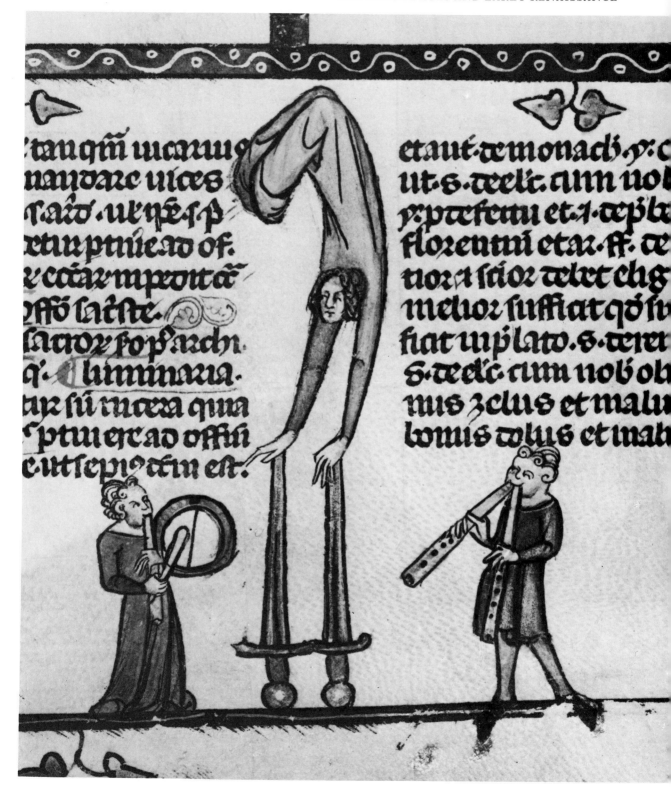

oïl, much as it is today, hence the other term, *langue d'oïl*. As there were two distinct linguistic and cultural groups in the Middle Ages, so there were two distinct secular musical traditions, and the troubadours of the south were followed by the much more prolific *trouvères* of the north. They had in common, however, their idealization of womanhood, in considerable contrast to the more worldly, more robust attitude of the goliards. Despite the secular context of their songs, there are strong religious overtones in their attitudes to love, doubtless influenced by the devotion to the Virgin Mary prevalent at this time.

If the spirit of the new songs was secular, many of their forms evolved from ecclesiastical chant, especially from hymns, litanies, and the sequence, which had been a further development in the liturgy in the intervening period. However, there were at least three very popular song forms that were not inspired by Church music, namely the *ballade, virelai* and *rondeau*. They were entirely secular, and probably had their origin in some early kind of dance-song. There were very similar movements in Spain and Italy, though unfortunately little or nothing has survived of the Italian output of that time. We can recapture the flavour of it, however, in the *laudi spirituali*, which were hymns sung on penitential pilgrimages, but which closely resemble the French *virelai*.

In Germany the troubadours and *trouvères* inspired the Min-nesinger, though whereas only some of the former were aristocrats, the latter were never of humble origin. In time they gave way to the Meistersinger, who were tradesmen and artisans, and were so well depicted by Wagner in his opera *Die Meistersinger von Nürnberg* (1862–7). Before leaving the German tradition, reference must be made to the *Geisslerlieder*, in some ways the equivalent of the Italian *laudi*, for the movement had been carried across the Alps, especially during the plague of 1348. However, the *Geisslerlieder* had a more lasting appeal than the *laudi*, and although they were banned by the Church authorities at the same time, they in fact survived longer.

Medieval instruments

The Church's decision to exclude musical instruments from religious ceremonies did not mean that no musical instruments existed in medieval churches. Indeed one cannot say categorically that Gregorian Chant was never, anywhere, accompanied. However, the surviving musical manuscripts do not indicate what instruments were to be used, nor indeed whether they were to be used at all. We must therefore rely for information on references in literature, decorations in illuminated manuscripts, carved ivory, metalwork and sculpture. During the early Middle Ages the organ had, after all, found its way into churches, although it was of limited use. Apart from its size and loudness, there was another considerable physical problem in that organs of this period had no keyboards (they were

Hans Sachs (1494–1576) flourished towards the end of the great period of the German *Meistersinger*, though in fact they survived until the nineteenth century in the city of Ulm. Sachs was not only a composer but also a poet and playwright.

Providing wind pressure for early organs was an athletic task. Here the bellows are trodden with the feet, and the blower holds on to a bar as he works, his tunic tucked into his belt to give him freedom of movement.

added only at the beginning of the thirteenth century), and were operated by cumbersome slides that had to be pushed and pulled to open and close the bottom of the pipes and thus control the wind supply. There were two smaller organs, however: one was the positive, which could be moved about but needed two people, one to blow and another to operate the slides, and both to carry it; the other was the portative, which could be carried by one person who could operate the bellows and the slides at the same time.

There were stringed instruments, too, the simplest of them being the monochord. As the name suggests, this consisted of a single string, and was traditionally thought to have been invented by Pythagoras (*c*.570–*c*.500 BC) in order to demonstrate his musical system. In the later Middle Ages it was bowed, but it can never have been a very flexible instrument, to say the least, and was therefore more suited to teaching than performing. Of the other plucked or struck stringed instruments, the harp and psaltery were both popular – much more popular, in fact, than the monochord. However, particularly attractive in view of the new music being written were the bowed stringed instruments, since they could give a sustained note as well as providing the flexibility necessary for rapid fingering.

The two most important of these were the rebec and the vièle or fiddle. The rebec was the smaller of the two, had fewer strings, and in some illustrations is shown held under the chin in a similar way to the modern violin. The vièle, on the other hand, was played in a vertical position on the lap, rather as viols are played still. It had five strings, the lowest of which was a drone, providing a noise like the bagpipe drone or the held pedal note on the organ. Both of them came from the East, as did several instruments at this time, brought back by Crusaders who had come into contact with Oriental culture.

Closely allied to the vièle was the organistrum or hurdy-gurdy – nothing to do with the much later barrel-organ, which is a totally different kind of instrument. Somewhat confusingly the organistrum is also known as the vielle. Basically, however, it was a stringed instrument that in its earlier versions required two players – one to

RIGHT An illustration of bagpipes from the Luttrell Psalter in the British Museum (c. 1340). The large trumpet-shaped pipe is in fact the drone, and the conical pipe with finger holes is the chanter, on which the tune is played.

BELOW The rebec was one of the earliest bowed, stringed instruments. Pegs hold the tension in the strings, which are inserted from the side.

turn a resined wheel to make the strings vibrate, and another to operate the wooden rods that stopped the strings and produced the different notes. In addition to the melody strings there were also drone strings. Later it was reduced in size so that one person could play it, and in this form, though refined and improved, it lasted until well into the eighteenth century, and even enjoyed aristocratic patronage in France.

Wind instruments also existed, of course. Of the flute family there were the recorder and related flageolet, as well as an early version of the transverse or side-blown flute. The reed family had the double-reed shawm, descended from the Greek *aulos*, and a forerunner of the oboe. There was also a wooden horn, known as the cornett – not to be confused with the brass instrument, which has only one 't'. Finally there were various percussion instruments, such as bells, drums, cymbals, and possibly tambourines. From this very varied array of tonal colour and timbre, one can see that the Early Church Fathers would probably have been amazed and shocked at what had happened, and even in the twelfth century not all clergy were happy at the turn things had now taken.

Other instruments were in use at this time, but do not seem to have found their way into churches. Of these the most important were the lute, the guitar, bagpipes, panpipes, horns and trumpets, and no doubt some percussion instruments such as the triangle and castanets. Surviving manuscripts do not tell us what instruments were to be played at any given moment, but imaginative modern realizations have revealed works to us in a way that would have been unimaginable only thirty or forty years ago.

Alongside this development of instrumental character, another had taken place in the structure of music itself that was to have a much more profound effect on Western music: this was the development of part-music, or polyphony as it is known.

The invention of part-music

Although the tradition of melody had been, from earliest times, for monophony or a single voice or part – and in this respect Gregorian Chant might be considered to be its perfect expression in the West – from the early Middle Ages a desire was also felt to sing in parts. There were two ways of doing this. One was parallel organum, in which the melody is repeated exactly and simultaneously, but at different pitches; its limitation, however, is that the tune can *only* be reproduced at different pitches. Another kind of organum, giving more scope, is called free organum, in which the second voice might move in parallel, oblique or contrary motion – in other words with the melody, away from it, or towards it.

All of this can be described in theoretical terms, but we ought to consider what it actually meant to the people of the time. They were used for so long to singing in unison or in octaves, that additional

ABOVE This bronze *lur* is in the Nationalmuseet in Copenhagen. Widely used throughout Scandinavia from the twelfth to the sixth century BC, it is thought that the *lur* may have been inspired by the horns of the mammoth.

RIGHT The gentle sonority of the handbell was often a happy addition to the pipe and tabor combination for dancing and games, and handbell ringing, with a range of bells, developed into a considerable art.

LEFT King Alfonso x (the Wise) of Spain gathered together a number of poems, some of which he wrote himself, known collectively as the *Cantigas de Santa Maria* (*c*. 1270), contained in two manuscripts now in the Escorial. Here we see a pair of long trumpets known in Spanish as *añafil*, decorated with banners bearing armorial insignia.

notes such as fourths or fifths must have sounded very new to them, and very rich in the harmonic sense, while thirds and sixths would have required an even greater adjustment. Today we happily accept chords that even our grandparents would have thought unbearably harsh, and we may have developed or extended our harmonic sense considerably, but whether we have at the same time improved it is a different matter. This may help to demonstrate why musicians were relatively slow to develop polyphony.

Music with more than one part, then, was the first step in the development of polyphony. The second and equally important step was independent movement in the rhythm. Parallel and free organum could never on their own have led the way forward, because the other parts would always be bound to the rhythm of the melody, or *cantus firmus*. Its Latin name explains what it really was – fixed and rock-like in music terms. At the beginning of the twelfth century the *cantus firmus* was being sung in long, held notes, while the second voice sang what was by now an apparently almost unrelated florid tune above it. Effectively, then, the upper part was singing several notes to the held note of the original melody, and this posed the problem of when the held or tenor note (from the Latin *tenere*, to hold) was to move on to the next one, since music was not yet divided up neatly into bars of equal or related duration. In practice the choirmaster probably gave some indication, and the problem may seem to us to be more acute, with our modern view of what constitutes ensemble, than it was for twelfth-century musicians. They might well have been content if the phrase began and ended on a musical concord, for example. The place where this rhythmic independence seems to have been most fully developed in the first half of the twelfth century – certainly it is the place about which we have most information – was the monastery of St Martial at Limoges in France. Another flourishing centre was at Santiago de Compostela in north-west Spain, the only part of that country not conquered by the Moors; the Compostela school was evidently under the influence of Limoges. Both these centres were to wane in importance, however, as the focus in France moved further north, to Paris, where the magnificent new cathedral of Notre Dame was begun in 1163.

The new cathedral became the centre of a musical tradition known as the school of Notre Dame, and for virtually the first time in polyphonic development we know the names of the composers. This may seem strange to us, who live in the post-Renaissance period, when the artist emerged supremely as an individual, but almost all the very early composers, writers and artists were monks or in some sort of holy orders, and had no conception of an artistic vocation. They simply fulfilled their role within their community, and had no concern about later problems such as freedom of expression or artistic integrity.

Two composers in particular are important at this time. They are known either by their Latinized names, as Leoninus and Perotinus, or in the vernacular, as Léonin and Pérotin. Léonin, who flourished c.1150–80, was really the bridge between the St Martial school and the full development of Pérotin's style, c.1180–1220. What the Notre Dame school achieved and what, as we have already seen, was most necessary, was the organization of music from the rhythmic point of view. They developed a system that gave accent and metre to the notes, and they divided their compositions into sections that were clearly defined. One specific practice, concerning the way they arranged the *cantus firmus* in the tenor into a series of patterns that were rhythmically alike, paved the way for one of the next great steps forward – the development of the form known as the motet. The motet had a longer life than almost any other form in the history of music so far – some five hundred years, up to the time of Bach. It outlasted the *conductus*, another important form which appeared more prominently during the twelfth century, and it was probably responsible for its decline. Unlike the organum, the *conductus* was a completely free piece of music, and the text, too, was usually a free composition. On the Continent its popularity lasted for little more than a century, until c.1250, though in modified forms it survived in Britain until the mid-fifteenth century.

To find an image that expresses what happened to music in this period, contrast the architectural style of that brand new Gothic cathedral of Notre Dame in Paris with the solid, eloquent, but earthbound Romanesque architecture that went before. Gothic architecture – at least in its first manifestation – was clear-cut and symmetrical, a unification of homogeneous component parts in which everything, including the ornamentation, was conceived as having and being subordinate to its place in the overall effect. When we compare it with the music of Pérotin, for example, with its clearly differentiated sections, distinctive rhythms and straightforward

BELOW Bladder pipes from the *Cantigas de Santa Maria*. The pipe with the flared end is the drone, and the shorter one, which is fingered, is the chanter.

RIGHT The cathedral of Notre Dame in Paris was the home of a remarkable school of composers and performers in the second half of the twelfth century who brought the music of the day to a high point in its development.

tunes, we become aware of remarkable points of similarity. Of course, this style of music did not sweep the whole of Europe. It is no coincidence, for example, that Italy, where the Gothic style of architecture never really took hold, did not produce a school of music similar to that of Notre Dame, and there were fundamental reasons, too, why even in France the Notre Dame style did not completely take over. Such music required a highly skilled, professional band of singers, who could not only sing the written notes, but could also provide extempory ornamentation of their line of music. Only the great cathedrals such as Notre Dame could attract and support such singers; indeed their presence was much more appropriate there than in the great monastic establishments, where Gregorian Chant still held sway in its pure form. Notre Dame represented the pinnacle – and a Gothic one at that – rather than the body of the building, which was still in a state of transition from Romanesque.

ABOVE The importance attached to music in the Middle Ages, and indeed throughout the history of Christianity, is reflected in the countless representations of the Virgin and Child in which angels sing and play instruments. In this illumination from a manuscript in the British Museum can be seen, among other instruments, a psaltery, a monochord, a harp, a portative organ, and a pipe and tabor.

LEFT A miniature from a manuscript in the Bibliothèque Nationale, Paris, illustrating the *chant royal* with which Nicole Levestu won the prize at the Puys de Rouen in 1523. The work concerned the composition of a motet for thirty-six voices by Jean d'Ockeghem, and the illustration depicts the performance of it.

Until the end of the twelfth century virtually all part music was written for the Church, and, generally speaking, any music outside the religious context – therefore secular – was monophonic. From the beginning of the thirteenth century monophony began to retreat, and part music was used for both sacred and secular contexts. There was, moreover, a universal style of music during the thirteenth century, a style created by Pérotin of the school of Notre Dame. It embraced Church music, the equivalent of the pop songs of the day, and dance music – a state of affairs that scarcely any subsequent period came anywhere near achieving. The medieval mind saw a unity in the universe and man's place in it that we seem unlikely ever to be able to translate into contemporary terms.

This comprehensive view is well demonstrated in the evolution of the motet. In one example the tenor has only one word, *veritatem* (truth), which together with its tune is taken from the Gradual for the Feast of the Assumption of the Blessed Virgin Mary, beginning with the Latin words *Propter veritatem*. Two voices sing in parts above the tenor phrase, which is repeated twice, but each of these voices sings a different text in Latin. One of the upper tunes is in fact a troubadour song. Both texts are, however, a commentary on the Assumption, and as such an expansion of the truth with which the original tenor phrase is concerned. This combination of several sets of words is known as polytextuality; later examples combine more than one language, and even sacred and secular, with a Latin religious text in the tenor part and French secular texts in the upper parts.

If the result seems to us a somewhat incoherent jumble of sound, certain points must be borne in mind. Firstly, this music was not written for the general public. It was intended for a circle of musicians and clerics who understood the texts and the way in which the music was written. The motets may well have been performed as they were written, starting with the tenor, as a solo, then repeated by the tenor with one of the upper parts, and finally sung a third time, with all three parts together, with or without instruments. The result would therefore be a pleasing and stimulating synthesis offered to God as an act of worship. And it was through intellectual and emotional involvement, rather than through any active participation, that worship was offered.

Since Mozart's day, in fact, this technique has been commonly used in opera, where the process is taken a step further, for often operatic ensembles not only have different words and tunes but register differing emotions, so that the ensemble becomes a culmination of all the emotions displayed up to that point. It was the unified concept, the synthesis, that was the hallmark of thirteenth-century music, and which has made it, in the opinion of many people, among the greatest in Western musical history. Before the century had passed, however, a composer by the name of Philippe de Vitry (1291–1361) was born, and it was from his treatise *Ars nova* that the next development in music derived its name.

27

An illustration from an illuminated manuscript in the Bibliothèque Nationale, Paris, showing minstrels leading a wedding procession, their long trumpets hung with banners.

The new art

Since France had dominated European music to such a large extent and for so long, it was perhaps not surprising that the *Ars nova* or new art should be formulated in the works of two Frenchmen, Philippe de Vitry and his friend, the philosopher and mathematician Jean de Muris (*Ars novae musicae – The New Art of Music* – 1319). However, the most influential figure in French music in the fourteenth century was Guillaume de Machaut (*c.*1304–77). Born in Champagne in northern France, he was educated to the priesthood, but at the age of twenty or so he became secretary to King John of Bohemia, whom he followed around Europe in the course of his military exploits. After the King was killed at the Battle of Crécy in 1346, Machaut worked at the French court, and pursued his career as a canon of Rheims Cathedral. Machaut's great achievement in musical history was the unification of the various different aspects of the *Ars nova*, which he combined into a recognizable style. He was also a poet of considerable talent.

One of Machaut's most important contributions was his extensive use of isorhythm or equal rhythm, which was a way of giving unity to a long composition that otherwise might have no formal organization.

A detail from *The Church Militant and Triumphant*, Andrea da Firenze's decoration of the Spanish Chapel of the Church of Santa Maria Novella in Florence. In this section are depicted the pleasures and vanities of the world. In the upper register on the left is a bowed, five-stringed, waisted fiddle, and in the lower register a bagpipe with its drone; on the right is a tambourine with jingles.

This does not mean that it was immediately recognizable as such – in fact more often than not it must have been undetected by the listener, but then, as we have already seen in the case of the motet, it was precisely this kind of feature that appealed to the medieval mind. Machaut was not by any means the first to use isorhythm, but no one had previously applied it in this way. Although the majority of his music that has survived is secular – oddly enough – the work that most stands out is his setting of the Mass, often known as the *Messe de Notre Dame*. Possibly composed for the coronation of Charles v in 1364, the work is rather conservative in tone, considering how late in Machaut's career it was written. Some music historians feel that for this reason it may have been written earlier than 1364, but Charles had been a patron of Machaut in the past, and it is quite likely that for so solemn an occasion Machaut would in any case have written a rather more conservative work.

Be that as it may, in another respect the work was almost a century ahead of its time, in that it was the first complete setting of the Ordinary of the Mass by one known composer. Machaut's Mass stands alone for its technical accomplishment, its great vigour and its inventiveness. Indeed, one might go even further and look upon it as

29

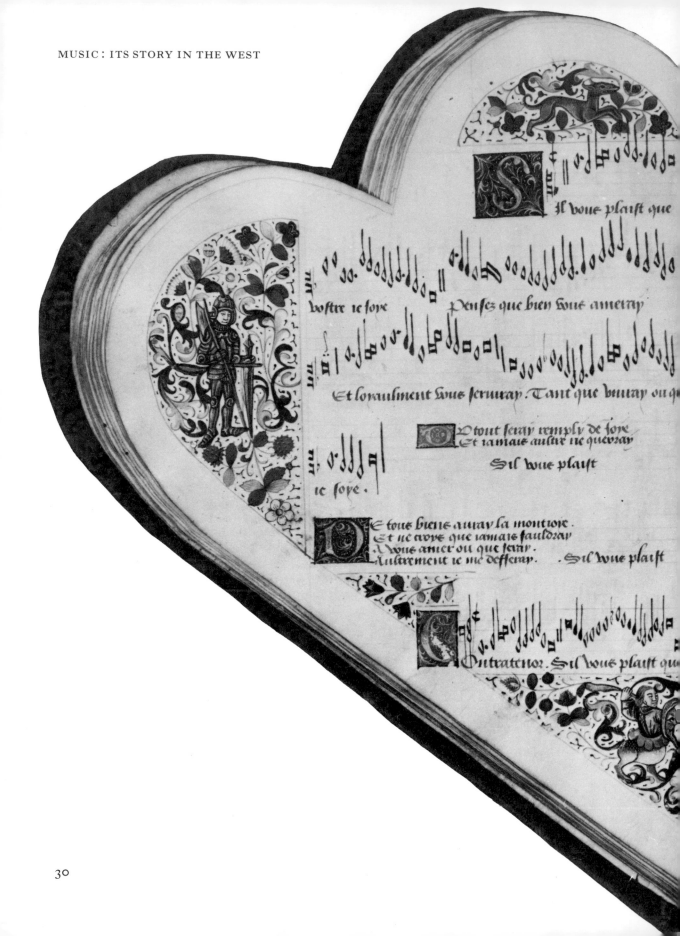

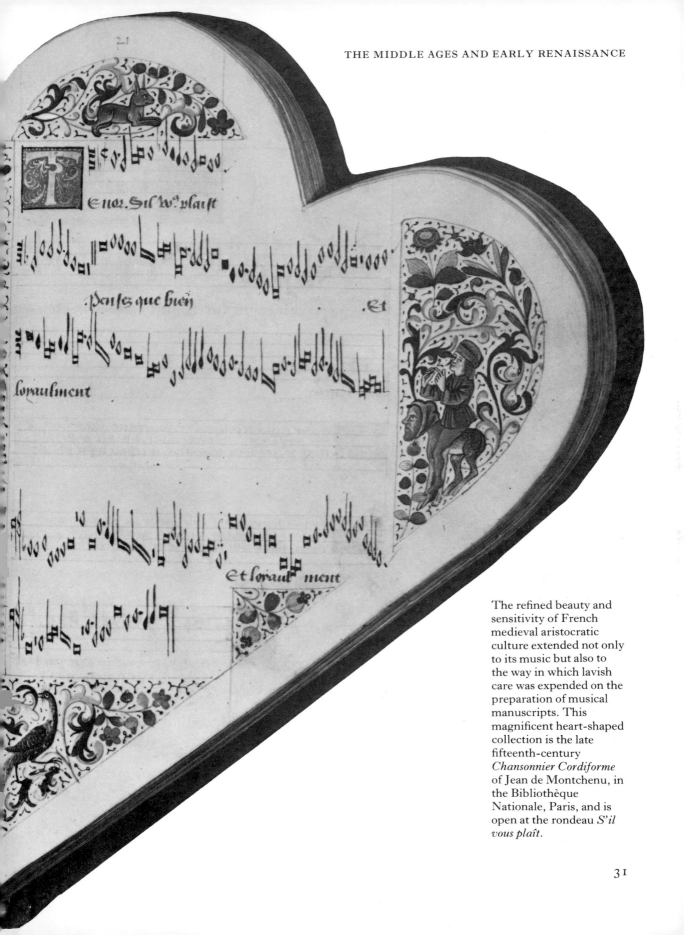

The refined beauty and sensitivity of French medieval aristocratic culture extended not only to its music but also to the way in which lavish care was expended on the preparation of musical manuscripts. This magnificent heart-shaped collection is the late fifteenth-century *Chansonnier Cordiforme* of Jean de Montchenu, in the Bibliothèque Nationale, Paris, and is open at the rondeau *S'il vous plaît*.

a distillation of the characteristics of the *Ars nova* in France. It has the jazz-like effect of syncopation and hocket (where the tune is sung in short notes with rests or gaps between each note, or is actually split between two voices – a device that especially exasperated some of the clergy); it also has rich and elaborate tunes, the setting of words by syllable, the incorporation of Gregorian tenor parts in addition to ones Machaut composed himself, the use of a chant in an elaborated form in an upper part, and the use of instrumental accompaniment.

Machaut had many followers and imitators; his style was taken outside France by French composers as far south as Aragon, and there was an important centre at Avignon in south-eastern France where the Popes resided between 1305 and 1378. With the Black Death, the Hundred Years' War, and rival claimants for the Papacy, this was hardly a period of strength and confidence for the Church. Moreover, in an attempt to keep religious music within prescribed limits, the ecclesiastical authorities discouraged composers from writing for the Church and from putting their talents at her disposal. The royal courts contained plenty of rulers and aristocrats prepared to welcome musicians and act as their patrons; and it was much easier for composers to pursue their new ideas in an ambiance that was free from the restrictions imposed by the Church. This also shows how times had changed. Whereas, before, composers had felt no incentive to draw away from the Church, now they not only felt a very powerful incentive, but at the same time had become aware of themselves as creators.

When we turn to consider Italy and the *Ars nova* we are struck at once by the absence of religious music. Indeed, there has been a tendency to undervalue the whole of the Italian contribution, or at best to regard it as an extension of the French. For one thing, though there were Italian composers of note between about 1325 and 1425, they left no school behind them, and the rest of the fifteenth century represents something of a musical void. In some respects, however, the later Italian *Ars nova* excelled that of the French, in spite of the fact that the country was torn by strife and was in any case highly fragmented because of the rivalry of the various small states which it comprised. Composers were to be found in a number of cities, especially in the north, for instance Bologna, Padua, Genoa, Rimini and Florence, and also further south, at Perugia and Caserta.

Italian music of the *Ars nova* was, it is true, deeply influenced by that of France, but in one particular aspect – melody – it managed to assert its own personality. This is seen at its best in the form of the madrigal – not, it must be stressed, in the sixteenth-century Renaissance madrigal, which was something very different, but in the fourteenth-century Italian madrigal which was essentially a verse form, often only of two parts; it had clarity and elegance, as well as providing the opportunity for the voices to be heard in a way that the later madrigal did not permit. The form of music known as the *caccia* had a French counterpart, but the Italian version, in which the two

Francesco Landini (1325–97), although blind from childhood, was so eminent a performer on the portative organ that it was deemed a fitting tribute to the man and his talent to depict him in this way on his tombstone. Note the angel instrumentalists in the top corners.

upper voices sang the same tune in canon, slightly out of step with each other, had a distinctive character, and the subject matter was not limited to hunting, as the name might suggest, but might also describe market scenes, or even a house catching fire. The third type of secular music at this time in Italy was the *ballata*, which was closely associated with the dance.

The composer who stands out far beyond all other fourteenth-century Italian musicians was Francesco Landini (1325–97). As a boy he lost his sight as a result of smallpox, but by sheer determination he mastered his disability and became a well-educated man, a poet of distinction, an expert on the theory and practice of music, and a skilled performer, especially on the organ. He wrote madrigals, *cacce* and *ballate*, but although he is known to have composed motets, none has survived in a form complete enough for us to be able to gain any very accurate impression of them. The lack of surviving religious output in Landini's work is typical of his time, and we know more about his organ-playing in a secular context than we do in a religious one.

The whole subject of instrumentation in this period remains hard to define. We know, for example, that the earliest clavichords and harpsichords were invented at this time, possibly in Britain, though they did not come into common use until the next century. Similarly, organs were being introduced into churches more and more, and additions were made to them all the time. Towards the end of the fourteenth century pedal boards appeared in Germany, and early in the fifteenth century stop mechanisms, which enabled the player to select different ranks of pipes, were introduced, as was a second keyboard. There is still room for discussion as to which instruments were used at any given time, however, or even whether some pieces were envisaged as vocal or instrumental, or a mixture of both. The very fact that no one bothered to make any indication on the manuscripts implies that it was more a question of availability. We must also bear in mind that at this time homogeneous timbre, such as that provided by a consort of viols, for example, had not yet evolved, and the taste was still for mixtures of fairly contrasting tonal colour, so that one might well find a viol, a lute, a psaltery, a flute and a drum playing together. This is an indication that the medieval concept of the role and nature of music was one of unity in diversity.

Apart from passing references, English music seems to have been rather neglected so far. This does not mean that there was none, but it had hitherto been somewhat out of the main stream of European music – though less so perhaps than was usually thought by scholars in the past. It had produced at least one composition, the *Reading Rota*, known better, perhaps, as '*Sumer is i-cumen in*', which was technically ahead of its time, and which cannot have been an isolated example, even if it is the only one to have survived. There was also the very special tradition of the carol, which was by no means restricted to Christmas. English musicians were known to like strong sonority

LEFT Two musicians from a fresco in the Tomb of the Leopards (*c.* 480–70 BC) from Tarquinia in Italy. These Etruscan figures provide a link between early practice and subsequent Roman developments. On the left can be seen double reed pipes or *tibia*, and on the right a lyre.

BELOW A mosaic from Pompeii by Dioscorides of Samos, in the National Museum at Naples, depicting Roman street musicians of the first century BC. From left to right the instruments are double pipes, small cymbals and frame drum.

ABOVE A detail from *The Triumph of the Church over the Synagogue* (also known as *The Fountain of Life*) by a pupil or follower of Jan van Eyck, in the Prado, Madrid. The instruments are a bowed fiddle, a portative organ and a monochord on the left, and on the right a psaltery, a lute played with a plectrum, and a harp.

LEFT The Reading Rota (*c.* 1226), better known by its opening words 'Sumer is i-cumen in', may be a folk song in origin, but in this form is a sophisticated composition for six voices, and probably the first example of musical canon as a form in its own right.

in their music, an effect created by the use of certain intervals such as thirds and sixths which, as we have already seen, were regarded with a certain amount of distrust on the Continent because of the acoustic problems they presented.

One factor that created a fundamental difference from their Continental counterparts was that British composers had the ecclesiastical Sarum (the old name for Salisbury) liturgical rite with its own tunes, on which they based their compositions, and this varied in certain ways from the Roman rite. Also unlike Continental composers, British composers, judging from the music that has survived, still devoted almost all their talents to religious music, and hardly bothered with secular compositions. The music school attached to Worcester Cathedral is known to have particularly flourished, and another focal point was the Chapel Royal. These concentrations of musical activity are important, because when a composer of the stature of John Dunstable appeared, he was obviously not an isolated phenomenon but the product of a strong tradition.

Dunstable (d.1453) took his name from the Bedfordshire town, with its ancient priory. His date of birth is unknown – it was probably in the latter part of the fourteenth century. It is possible that he learnt to sing as a member of the Chapel Royal, and then took orders and

RIGHT The Troparium of St Martial (*c.* 1100) in the Bibliothèque Nationale, Paris, not only records the plainsong melodies of the time but also illustrates performers such as this juggler accompanied by a double-reed pipe.

FAR RIGHT The York Psalter (*c.* 1175) in the University Library, Glasgow, shows King David tuning his harp, while above him a bell chime is played, at his feet is a rebec player, on the right a waisted fiddle is bowed on the lap and in the centre left is a triple duct flute. In the bottom rondels are handbells and psaltery, and a two-man organistrum.

ABOVE Instrumentalists from the thirteenth-century Spanish *Cantigas de Santa Maria*, with a rebab (a version of the rebec) and a large nine-stringed lute. They show how strong was the influence of the Middle East on the development of Spanish music, an influence that was ultimately to spread throughout much of Western Europe.

LEFT Dufay and Binchois, with portative organ and harp, from the fifteeenth-century *Champion des Dames* in the Bibliothèque Nationale, Paris.

OVERLEAF:
ABOVE LEFT Pipe and tabor players from the *Cantigas de Santa Maria* in the Escorial, Spain.

BELOW LEFT The Glory Portal of the cathedral at Santiago de Compostela in Spain shows Christ in glory flanked by the four evangelists and the instruments of the Passion. Even when working in stone, medieval artists felt that angelic choirs and instrumentalists were a necessary part of any representation of divine glory, and here carved a fine array of stringed instruments.

RIGHT Filippino Lippi (*c.* 1457–1504) was clearly inspired by ancient Roman instruments for the horn (known as a *cornu*) and the lyre in this painting, though the two forms of trumpet owe something to artistic licence. Also shown are a tambourine with jingles, and small drums and drumsticks. The subject is the worship of the Egyptian bull god, Apis.

became a canon of Hereford Cathedral. He entered the service of the Duke of Bedford, brother of King Henry V, who was regent in France from 1422 to 1435, commanding the armies fighting against Joan of Arc. This is no doubt one of the reasons why most of Dunstable's music that has come down to us has been found on the Continent; only one piece – without an attribution, moreover – appears in the Old Hall manuscript, the chief source for English music of this period, which once belonged to St George's Chapel, Windsor Castle. Of course it is dangerous to draw conclusions from relatively small selections of the musical output of any one period, but British composers had considerable influence at this time, and their love of sonorities was important in the struggle that was going on between the contrapuntal and the harmonic principles. This means, in essence, the tension – to some extent ever-present in the history of style in music – between the independence of the melodic line as opposed to the overall effect of the harmony. The progression throughout the whole of the medieval period was, in the very broadest terms, towards the harmonic principle. In this process, English influence was important. As the French poet Martin le Franc wrote *c.*1441: 'They wear the English guise gracefully and follow Dunstable, whereby they have learnt to make their music bright and gay.' 'They' in this context refers to Dufay and Binchois, who were the two leading composers on the Continent at that time, and in particular of the Burgundian school.

The dukes of Burgundy were theoretically vassals (in the strictly feudal sense) of the kings of France. Their territory originally centred on Dijon, in central eastern France, but while the Hundred Years' War was raging between France and England the Burgundians built up their power and territory to the point where the vassal virtually eclipsed his lord. It was not until 1477 that there was any considerable reduction in the size of the Burgundian domain, and a further five years before the duchy was reunited to the French crown. At its height it stretched from Dijon northwards through Lorraine and Luxembourg, across what is now north-eastern France, and into present-day Belgium and Holland. Both Dufay and Binchois were born in the province of Hainaut, on the Franco-Belgian border, in the heart of the Burgundian state, around 1400. Binchois died at the age of sixty, but Dufay lived on to seventy-four. They flourished, therefore, during the reign of Philip the Good (1396–1467; reigned from 1419), a generous patron of musicians. Although Dufay was a choirboy at Cambrai, it is not known for certain that he was ever a member of the ducal chapel, but from 1428 until 1433 he was a member of the papal chapel in Rome; he then spent some time in the service of the Duke of Savoy before returning to the papal chapel for a while, and ultimately to Cambrai. His music is known to have been performed at the Burgundian court, however, especially during the Feast of the Pheasant which took place in 1454.

Binchois we know was in the service of Philip the Good, certainly

from about 1430 until his death, and his *chansons* capture in their gentle, lyrical melancholy something of an age that was passing. Though both composers wrote *chansons*, Binchois's seem the more charming. There was a much more cerebral quality in Dufay's music, and it will perhaps be no surprise to learn that he wrote a motet for the consecration of Florence Cathedral in 1436 in which the overall rhythmic proportions of the various sections, as well as some other details, correspond exactly to the proportions of Brunelleschi's dome. Again, there is no complete surviving setting of the Mass by Binchois, whereas one of Dufay's most impressive works is the Mass *L'Homme armé*, where the *cantus firmus* is no longer a chant but a popular song – a tradition that became more and more prevalent, and continued into the fifteenth and sixteenth centuries. For this, and various technical considerations, some scholars regard Binchois and Dufay, and Dunstable too, not as composers of the late Middle Ages but as heralds of the Renaissance.

The cathedral square in Florence, with its free-standing campanile and baptistry, was always a perfect setting for processions on the great festivals of the Church's year, when magnificent music was lavished on the ceremonial. This painting in the Palazzo Vecchio, Florence, is by one of the followers of Giorgio Vasari (1511–74).

ABOVE For the
consecration of Florence
Cathedral in 1436, Dufay
wrote a motet whose
proportions corresponded
exactly to those of
Brunelleschi's
magnificent dome, which
still dominates much of
the surrounding city and
countryside.

Renaissance means literally rebirth, and it is true that in many fields of art, especially in painting, sculpture and architecture, there was a rebirth of artistic endeavour, particularly after the Fall of Constantinople; it was stimulated by the rediscovery of ancient classical works of art and literature. In music, however, there were no discoveries that were in any way comparable, since what had been known from classical antiquity had been handed down from generation to generation, right through the medieval period. What is true is that once the Renaissance gained momentum, music was affected by the spirit of the times, and theorists attempted to revive classical traditions, to the extent that opera was eventually created. In general terms music evolved in response to other developments that were much more deeply rooted in civilization in its broadest sense, and therefore initially the Renaissance was of less importance to music than to almost any other art form.

Angel musicians (*c.* 1480) by Hans Memling in the Koninklijk Museum voor Schone Kunsten, Antwerp.

These are the outer panels of a triptych, the central panel of which depicts Christ in the act of giving benediction. They are of particular interest for the iconography of the musical instruments of the time. From left to right the instruments are:

psaltery, tromba marina, lute, folded trumpet and tenor shawm on the left hand panel, and straight slide trumpet, folded slide trumpet, portative organ, harp with brays, and waisted fiddle with comb bridge on the right hand panel.

The tromba marina is the only stringed instrument on which the notes are produced by touching the string to produce natural harmonics, and is bowed

above the stopping finger; the fiddle at far right, for example, is bowed between the stopping finger and the bridge.

The brays on the harp are L-shaped pegs used to pin the strings into the belly of the instrument, while the horizontal arm touches the string and produces a buzzing sound, increasing both the volume and the sustaining power. It is in details such as this that Memling's paintings are so useful. Their exact purpose and provenance is still not entirely certain, but it is thought that they came from the abbey church of Santa Maria la Real at Najera in Castille, and that they decorated the front of the organ loft there.

2. The Renaissance

Flemish composers and the attraction of Italy

'The world is coming to its senses as if waking from a deep sleep', said Erasmus, describing the phenomenon of the Renaissance, and for music in particular the image of an awakening is a better one than that of rebirth. Where exactly one places the Renaissance as far as music is concerned is somewhat arbitrary. The period from 1450 to 1600 gains general acceptance, though some would put the beginning earlier, at 1420 or even before.

In 1475 the contemporary theorist Johannes Tinctoris (c.1435–1511) felt that virtually no music that was worth listening to had been written before 1440, and the Swiss Heinrich Loris, or Glareanus as he is known (1488–1563), wrote in his *Dodecachordon* of 1547 that no one would ever write better music than Josquin des Prés, who had died in 1521. Each generation seemed to have its own views on the matter. For example the Italian Gioseffo Zarlino (1517–90), who spent most of his life in Venice, thought that the Flemish composer Adrian Willaert (c.1490–1562), choirmaster at St Mark's, was beyond compare, and in the last decade of the sixteenth century the composers then active in Florence believed that they wrote the best music of their day, and that they had given new life to ancient Greek music. It is clear, whether strictly speaking there was a Renaissance in music or not, that the spirit of the age inspired musicians with confidence and optimism.

Certainly there must have been more music-making – of all sorts – than at any time previously in the West. This was accompanied by more freedom for composers. They did not yet enjoy total freedom, for they still depended very much on patronage from the Church and royal and aristocratic masters, but they had more room for experiment, and the composer was beginning to emerge as a much more important personality in his own right. The printing of music at the turn of the sixteenth century greatly facilitated the performance, even the very knowledge, of music in many cases, and so assured its greater dissemination. A wealth of informative books appeared

A detail from Gaudenzio Ferrari's decorations in Saronno Cathedral, Italy, dating from around 1535, showing, on the right, what is possibly the earliest representation of the violin as we know it. In the foreground is a viol, and on the left a lute, with cymbals behind. The instruments in the centre are somewhat fanciful.

ABOVE The composer Adrian Willaert (*c.* 1490–1562) depicted in a woodcut from *Musica nota* of 1559. Although he was a Fleming, Willaert spent much of his life in Venice, and enjoyed an international reputation in his own lifetime.

LEFT An ivory carving (*c.* 1620), now in the Bayerisches Nationalmuseum, by the Munich court artist Christof Angermaier. In the left foreground is a bass recorder, with a cornett and a racket behind. In the background are a crumhorn, pommer and transverse flute, and on the right panpipes, trombone and descant pommer.

(though this was a phenomenon of the times and by no means confined to music), and accomplishment in music became a part of every cultivated person's education.

Perhaps one of the most striking figures of the Renaissance was Johannes Ockeghem, or Jean D'Ockeghem (*c*.1425–95). After a period in the choir of Antwerp Cathedral he entered the service of the kings of France, and was employed by three successive monarchs: Charles VII, Louis XI and Charles VIII. When he died his fame was so great that he was mourned all over Europe. His religious music surpasses the rest, but the characteristic of all his work was his feeling for melody. If Ockeghem was a great composer, however, a greater one was yet to come, and it is no coincidence that the lament written by the French poet Jehan Molinet on the death of Ockeghem was set to music by Josquin des Prés (*c*.1450–1521), yet another product of Hainaut. Not only was he the greatest composer of the early Renaissance, but probably one of the greatest composers of all time. The very fact that we can even contemplate using such words shows, apart from anything else, how far we have now come down the path leading from the Middle Ages to the Renaissance.

Josquin spent a great deal of his working life in Italy, especially in Milan, Rome and Ferrara, and settled in France for the fifteen or sixteen years before his death. Some eighteen Masses by him survive, together with a hundred motets and seventy *chansons*, as well as other secular vocal works. He showed a somewhat conservative trait in his

IOSQVINVS PRATENSIS.

ABOVE A woodcut portrait of Josquin des Prés (*c*. 1450–1521).

RIGHT Franchino Gaffurio (1451–1522), appointed Master of Music at Milan Cathedral in 1484, was an ordained priest as well as musician and theorist, and published his *Practicae Musicae* in 1496.

Mass settings – even to the extent of using the tune *L'Homme armé* as a *cantus firmus* as others had done – but that is not perhaps surprising, since the Latin text was naturally sacrosanct, which always severely limits any composer's scope. For a Mass to be suitable for liturgical use, it must rigorously adhere to certain norms and gain ready acceptance by its users. For this reason composers have always had to be very careful when breaking new ground, which has tended to result in conservatism. This does not mean that there was any lack of technical ingenuity in Josquin's Mass settings, but the large proportion of motets to anything else in his work indicates the source of the best examples of his genius.

Naturally he had contemporaries, and some distinguished ones, such as Jacob Obrecht (1450–1505), Heinrich Isaac (*c*.1450–1517), Pierre de la Rue (d.1518) and Jean Mouton (d.1522), who was the teacher of Adrian Willaert. As we have already seen, there was an increasing tendency for Flemish composers to go south to Italy, a trend which had begun during Josquin's lifetime, and of which he himself was an example, though the effects of the migration – principally a rising generation of native Italian composers – did not begin to be apparent until after his death. Not all composers were drawn to Italy, however. Nicholas Gombert (*c*.1500–*c*.1556) went to Madrid, and Philippe de Monte (1521–1603) to Prague. However, in view of the way in which Italy took up Flemish composers and their music, and in a subsequent generation became itself the seedbed of new musical developments, it is with Italy that we shall be primarily concerned.

Perhaps the best illustration of the process of Flemish migration is the career of Adrian Willaert, who went to Venice in 1527, remained there for the rest of his life and gained the coveted appointment of choirmaster at St Mark's. Under his inspiration Venice became a centre of forward-looking music. He was helped in this by the fact that Venice was fiercely independent, and there was something in the Venetian temperament that encouraged a certain daring, which the Romans would not have tolerated. The very nature of St Mark's, with its two choir galleries, each with an organ, was also a contributory factor. The church was really the Doge's private chapel, and only became the cathedral church of Venice much later, on the orders of Napoleon. If St Mark's lacked technical cathedral status until then, the brilliance of its music certainly made up for it.

Naturally musicians were attracted to Venice, and to Willaert in particular. Cipriano de Rore (1516–65), the creator of the classical madrigal, came there from the Netherlands, despite his Italian-sounding name, and another important figure, to whom we shall return, was the German Heinrich Schütz. Among the last of the long succession of Flemish musicians who went to Italy was Roland de Lassus, or Orlando di Lasso (1532–94). He became choirmaster to the Duke of Bavaria in Munich at the age of twenty-four, by which time he had already visited Milan, Naples, Rome, France, Antwerp,

Orlando di Lasso (or Roland de Lassus), born in 1532, was Flemish but travelled extensively throughout Europe before settling in Munich, where he died in 1594.

OVERLEAF For many years visitors were attracted to Venice from north of the Alps, not only for the richness of its buildings and ceremonial life but also for the excellence of its music and the opportunities it provided for musicians. This painting of a procession in the Piazza di San Marco is by Gentile Bellini (*c.* 1429–1507), and is in the Accademia, Venice.

and possibly England. He thus personified most of European musical culture, especially after his arrival in Munich, when he assimilated the trends that were current there too. But as ever, when the tide was at its fullest, it was also very near the turn, and having brought their gifts to foreign shores, the Flemish composers retreated; the next generation saw a rise of the national schools that these musicians had done so much to inspire.

England in isolation

England in the fifteenth and sixteenth centuries was once more somewhat isolated from the main stream. One reason for this was the internal strife during the Wars of the Roses (1455–85), and another

the fact that Dunstable's influence was mostly felt abroad, and benefited his own country little. Moreover England occupied a very much smaller place in the cultural world than it does today, and the only musical establishments of any note, apart from the Chapel Royal, were those of the great religious foundations and colleges, which were bound in any case to be very traditional. No sooner had the country begun to settle down under the Tudor dynasty than the religious turmoil that saw the dissolution of the monasteries and the reorganization of many of the cathedral and collegiate foundations was unleashed. This caused considerable administrative upheavals, though some composers were able to continue their work.

The *Eton Choirbook* (1490–1502) is presumably an indication of the sort of music sung at Henry VI's foundation there, though about half the original contents are missing or damaged. However, from what remains it is clear that the music was already old-fashioned for its time. The most notable composers featured in it are William Cornysh (d.1523) and Robert Fayrfax (1464–1521). The latter was responsible for the music performed by the English at the Field of the Cloth of Gold in 1520, when Henry VIII met François I of France near Calais in a somewhat pointless diplomatic extravaganza. Also performed on that occasion, according to tradition, was the Mass *Gloria tibi Trinitas* by John Taverner (c.1495–1545), who was possibly the greatest English composer of this period. His *Western Wynde* Mass was rather like *L'Homme armé* in its use of a popular tune, though Taverner's treatment was very different. When the suppression of the monasteries began, Taverner abandoned his musical career and joined in with zeal. Henceforth English Church music was to follow the bewildering changes of the English religion for the rest of the sixteenth century. Only a composer of the stature of Thomas Tallis (c.1505–85) was able to surmount the various obstacles and write music that skilfully married the vocal line to the words, blending the texture, creating a truly vocal style, and conveying the emotion of the text in a way that no other English composer did at the time, apart from William Byrd (1543–1623). It is notable that both Tallis and Byrd, however, were much more at ease with Latin texts than they were with English ones.

Some people regard Byrd as a composer even more highly than Tallis, and certainly, in view of his much wider output in both religious and secular music, Byrd merits attention. He wrote some remarkable keyboard music, for example. There was a considerable English tradition of keyboard music by this time, as we can deduce from this late flowering at the end of the sixteenth century, and from the music of Hugh Aston (c.1480–1522), a contemporary of Fayrfax. To some extent the same was true of the lute, for the English produced a rich school of lutenists towards the end of the sixteenth century. It is not surprising that there is no earlier corpus of instrumental music in England, for this also applies to Continental Europe, the exception being Germany where instrumental tech-

RIGHT Spinet lid in the Germanisches Nationalmuseum, Nuremberg, painted by Friedrich von Falckenberg c. 1615. It shows a consort of four viols accompanied by a spinet and organ combined. Note the different positions of the hands on the bows of the two upper instruments and the two bass instruments.

BELOW Musically speaking there is little difference between a spinet and virginals other than that between one make of piano and another, but the term spinet was reserved for the wing-shaped instrument illustrated below, and the term virginals for the rectangular instrument on page 77.

niques (and indeed the whole status of instrumentalists) were more advanced. It would be wrong to form the impression that there was suddenly considerably more instrumental music than ever before, however; it was simply that developments were taking place that put more emphasis on instruments and their performers, and more instrumental music was preserved as a result. One has only to look at the illustrations of everyday life that survive to realize that musical instruments were continuing in the role they had always had, but that it was expanding; one particular Renaissance development, for instance, was the complete family of instruments – known as the 'chest' or consort – which created new possibilities for ensemble. We must now look at the course taken by the various European countries at this time.

France, Germany, Spain and England

With the accession of François I (1515–47), France took on a new character. Gone were the quasi-independent states and the political anarchy of the Middle Ages. Instead a centralized government was formed, headed by a powerful monarch whose court was the focus of political, economic and artistic life. By the *Ordonnance de Villers-Cotteret*, François proclaimed that legal documents would no longer be written in Latin but in French; he founded the Collège de France and the National Press, and gave powerful impetus to the progress of the Renaissance in France by his military expeditions into Italy, and by bringing artists back to his court. The emphasis on the official use of the French language was important because when the French *chanson* began to develop on the foundation of the Italian *frottola*, it was essentially sung poetry, and not music with an added text. More than fifty collections of the new *chansons*, representing some 1,500 pieces, were published by Pierre Attaingnant between 1528 and 1552. The two most important composers in the early collections were Claudin de Sermisy (*c*. 1490–1562) and Clément Jannequin or Janequin (*c*.1485–*c*.1560). The latter, especially, wrote some spectacular extended pieces that imitate gossiping women (*Le caquet des femmes*), birdsong (*Le chant des oiseaux*), the hunt (*La chasse*) and armed combat (*La guerre*); the latter (of which there is a purely instrumental version too) was written to commemorate François I's victory over the Swiss at Marignano, which opened up the road to Milan for him, and it is said that when it was played at court the men drew their swords in salute.

By contrast with Janequin, the work of De Sermisy, as well as that of the later Claude le Jeune (1528–*c*.1600) and Guillaume Costeley (1531–1606), is much more suave and less extended, and we see in it the development that led eventually to the *air de cour*, in which the four-part setting of the earlier *chanson* had been modified to a single-voice part for soloist, and the three under-parts condensed into a lute

ABOVE The title page of
Pierre Attaingnant's
Second Book of Masses,
Paris 1532. The scene
shows a mass at the court
of François I (1515–47) at
the moment of the
elevation of the Host,
while the choir sings *O
salutaris hostia*.

accompaniment. By this point the text had become so important that
the melodic content of many of the *airs de cour* was overshadowed,
but it represented an important stage in the development towards the
solo music of the Baroque. A comparable situation can be seen in
England with the work of John Dowland (1563–1626), some of whose
airs were performed both as four-part vocal settings and as solo songs
with lute accompaniment. The melodic line was always more
important in English lute song, and did not suffer half so much as in
France.

The French religious music of this time shows little development
from the magnificent output of Josquin des Prés, and it would have
been hard for anyone to have surpassed him. Nevertheless one regrets
the lack of any sense of mysticism or passion, or even any very evident
feeling of devotion, in much of the post-Josquin French religious
music. It is all rather elegant and worldly, and little more than that.
There was one field, however, in which religious music achieved
distinction, and that was in the polyphonic setting of the Psalms
translated into French, in which a new breath of inspiration and
conviction can be felt. These settings were essentially a product of
Protestantism, and it was tragic that perhaps the greatest exponent of
them, Claude Goudimel (*c.*1510–72), was murdered with many
others in the Massacre of St Bartholomew's Eve.

The *chanson* remains the most characteristic product of the French Renaissance, but at the same time the way was opening up for the lute and harpsichord schools that were to flourish there in the next century, and the refinement of life at court heralded the development of the theatre through lavish dramatic ballet, which was a combination of verse, song, recitation and dance. Doubtless without a central monarchy this would not have taken place, and when we turn to Germany, we see that politico-religious considerations could play an equally important role in determining musical development.

In general the Renaissance was essentially an aristocratic or courtly movement, exclusive to a considerable degree, and certainly learned and artistic. Martin Luther's adherents in Germany formed essentially a middle-class movement, which only accepted those elements of the Renaissance – in particular learning – that could be used to support and further the practical and moral aims of the Reformation. Inevitably this resulted in a sober, restricted, even earthbound view of artistic life, in which joy was of a very restrained nature. Of course this chiefly describes Protestant northern Germany, whereas the Catholic south carried on its unbroken tradition from the Middle Ages.

Where Germany as a whole undoubtedly excelled was in its instrumental tradition, exemplified particularly in the work of Paul Hofhaimer (1495–1537), court organist to the Emperor Maximilian. He was the greatest organist of his day, and the teacher of many excellent musicians of the next generation. He was also an accomplished composer of *Lieder*, which were basically polyphonic songs, with a greater relationship to native melodic traditions, and even to folksong, than existed in the songs of most other European countries. *Lieder* continued to be published until the mid-sixteenth century, when they gave way to Italian influence, but by that time they had provided musical models for the hymns or chorales of the Lutheran Church.

By contrast the presence of such composers as Lassus in Munich, De Monte in Prague and Antonio Scandello (1517–80) in Dresden represented the other tradition, which led to the emergence of such composers as Jacob Handl, also known as Gallus (1550–91), and Hans Leo Hassler (1564–1612), as the Flemish and Italian schools (Venetian in the case of the latter) came to fruit in a more congenial soil. These Flemish and Italian influences also form part of the development of music in Spain.

Spain had its own equivalent of the Italian *frottola*, known as the *villancico*, of which one of the chief exponents at the start of the sixteenth century was Juan del Encina (1469–1529). However, considerable Flemish influence was exerted on Church music and polyphony generally from such men as Gombert, Manchicourt and Crecquillon, who all worked in Spain at some time. Nevertheless the Spanish character had some very different elements in it by comparison with France and Italy, and although a later-generation

ABOVE Hans Burgkmair's set of woodcuts known as the *Triumph of Maximilian* are an invaluable source of documentation for instruments of the early sixteenth century. Here we see Maximilian I's blind organist Paul Hofhaimer playing a positive organ.

ABOVE RIGHT From the same set of woodcuts, a broken consort of bass viol, harp, violin, mean lute and quintern (treble lute) with pipe and tabor on the right and, in the background, treble and tenor *rauschpfeife* (a kind of shawm).

LEFT Bronze gilt trumpet with decorated silver knobs made by Anton Schnitzer in Nuremberg in the sixteenth century.

composer such as Morales (*c*.1500–52) spent ten years in Rome as a member of the papal chapel, his music has a passionate quality that is quite Spanish, and which is also found in the music of Victoria (*c*.1550–1611) who takes it on to an even higher plane. Victoria may have studied with Palestrina (he succeeded him in the chair of music at the Collegium Romanum in 1571), but there is a quality in Victoria's music that is simply not present in Palestrina's, and which was entirely his own. Few have ever aspired to it subsequently, and indeed in the opinion of some he took *a cappella* (unaccompanied) polyphony to a level that no later composer has ever attained.

In the face of all this magnificent Church music, it would be easy to overlook the high degree of accomplishment of Spanish instrumental music of this period. Lute music in particular flourished to an extraordinary degree, but even now is paid scant attention compared with that of other European countries. Alonzo de Mudarra (d.1580) and Luis Milan (*c*.1500–61) were two of the better known composers, along with Miguel de Fuenllana (d.1579), who was blind. Another blind musician, Antonio de Cabezón (1510–66), may be taken as the representative of the attainment of Spanish keyboard music and technique at this time. A brilliant organist as well, Cabezón was a composer of great originality, both in his use of technical variation and in his bold use of chromaticism (the introduction of notes that normally would not occur in the key in which the music is written).

61

As a court musician to Philip II, he travelled to England in the royal entourage when the King married Mary Tudor. We also know from ambassadorial correspondence that other Spanish musicians were recruited in Spain for employment in England. By and large, however, the predominant foreign influence in English music in the second half of the sixteenth century tended to be Italian, and was destined to remain so for some time to come.

When we consider British music of this period, we must bear in mind that the two kingdoms of Scotland and England were still independent from one another. Because of the close links with the French court, Scottish music – especially the secular and religious music heard by the royal household – was heavily influenced by France. England was also receptive to foreign influence, in particular to that of Italy; in fact it tended to assimilate it more, and towards the end of the sixteenth century England developed its own tradition, mainly in the realm of secular vocal and instrumental music. In Church music, as we have already seen, religious upheavals made it difficult for a national style to emerge readily. In view of its importance as a source of influence, therefore, we must now turn to Italy itself, and see what had been taking place there, at the very heart of the European Renaissance.

ABOVE Orlando Gibbons (1583–1625), one of the greatest early seventeenth-century English musicians.

Italy

As the brilliant period of Italian music of the fourteenth and early fifteenth centuries declined, from about 1425 a host of northerners moved south. At times it seemed as if they would completely swamp the native talent, and certainly, by the mid-fifteenth century, manuscript music collections made in Italy might well contain more music by French, Flemish, and even English composers than by Italians. However, the potent influence of Italy itself began to make itself felt on the newcomers, and they passed on their musical knowledge and expertise to Italian pupils; by the end of the fifteenth century there were native composers once more, though their early efforts were by no means spectacular. The *frottola*, developed at Mantua at the court of Isabella d'Este, and Florentine carnival songs must be considered two of the most important elements, together with the French *chanson* (though that in turn had been influenced by the *frottola*), which combined to produce the next great development in music, and in Italian music in particular – the madrigal.

This new madrigal had nothing in common with the *Ars nova* madrigal, and indeed it is easier to say what the new madrigal was not rather than what it was, since it was a style, a genre, rather than a form as such. In the early stages of its existence it was more self-sufficient than it became later, when this elegant but not too complex music was used to interpret the meaning of the words of a poem. It is symptomatic of the state of musical life in Italy in the first thirty years or so of the sixteenth century that the three leading exponents were a

RIGHT The title page from Andrea Antico's first book of *Frottole intabulate da sonare organi*, which was published in Rome in 1517 and was the first printed organ tablature in Italy.

BELOW Although generally associated with Spain, the guitar has long been appreciated in France: this group of eight were a feature of the seventeenth-century court ballet *Les Fées da la Forêt de Saint Germain*.

Part of the Capirola lute book, now in the Newberry Library, Chicago. Vincenzo Capirola (1474–*c.* 1548) was a Venetian nobleman, lutenist and composer. This lute book, with beautiful illuminated borders, was probably produced around 1517, and is a landmark in Italian composition.

Frenchman, an Italian and a Fleming. They were, respectively, Philippe Verdelot (d.*c*.1540), Costanzo Festa (d.1545) and Jacques Arcadelt (*c*.1504–after 1567). As a measure of Arcadelt's popularity, his first book of madrigals was reprinted about thirty-three times up till 1654. Most of these were written in Rome, where Festa also worked, though in 1553 Arcadelt settled in France, where he turned to the *chanson*. Verdelot worked in Florence and published in Venice, and it was in Venice that Willaert, whom we have already encountered, also excelled in the form of the madrigal.

It was in fact one of Willaert's pupils, Cipriano de Rore from the Netherlands, who carried forward the next stage of the madrigal's development. Rore's northern temperament may go a long way towards accounting for the extraordinary intensity that he introduced into music in order to convey the inner sense of the text, rather than simply to illustrate it. Rore's influence can be traced through another Netherlander who spent most of his life in Italy, Giaches de Wert (1535–96), and Orlando di Lasso. Although di Lasso is perhaps more important as a composer of religious music, he wrote over 270 madrigals – almost three times as many as Rore. A strong claimant to being Rore's emotional successor, however, was Philippe de Monte, who produced the staggering total of more than a thousand madrigals of one kind or another.

Another composer more noted for his religious music than his madrigals is Palestrina (1524/5–94; his real name was Giovanni Pierluigi – Palestrina was the name of his home town). Yet he wrote more madrigals than Rore – about 150 of them – and was not on the whole influenced by him. Palestrina was based in Rome, but at the top of the Italian peninsula, in far-off Venice, was another madrigalist – or at least writer of madrigals, since his importance and influence came about chiefly through his instrumental music – Andrea Gabrieli (*c*.1520–86). Like Rore, Gabrieli was a pupil of Willaert, and was associated with St Mark's in Venice. The man who summed up virtually all that had gone before in the madrigal, however, was Luca Marenzio (1553–99), who went to Warsaw at one stage in his career, but spent most of his working life in Rome, Florence, Venice and Ferrara. Marenzio took word painting to its greatest heights, and later chromaticism reached its peak in the madrigals of the strange and tormented Carlo Gesualdo, Prince of Venosa (*c*.1560–1613). By way of contrast to the passion of Gesualdo, the madrigal comedies of Orazio Vecchi (1550–1605) display a much lighter touch, and led on to similar works by Adriano Banchieri (1567–1634) and Monteverdi, but by that time music had moved from the Renaissance to the Baroque, and we must leave that development until later.

Although it was mentioned earlier that many of these composers were also Church musicians, in Palestrina's case that statement cannot be left unqualified, for when we look at the Roman school in its historical perspective all that had gone before seems to have been

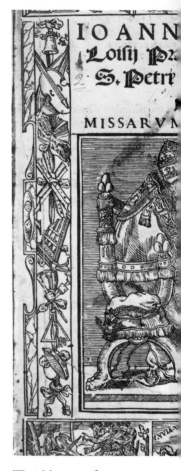

The title page of Palestrina's first book of Masses (1554) which is in the library of the Santa Cecilia Conservatory in Rome. Palestrina is shown presenting his works to his patron Pope Julius III.

leading to Palestrina; so brilliant was the style he perfected that it became the classic example of sixteenth-century contrapuntal composition. Of course Rome, being the seat of the Papacy, set the tone for the whole of Catholic Christendom as far as religious music was concerned, and was in a position to dictate its direction, but there was always a rival claimant when it came to sheer magnificence and splendour, and that was Venice, the Queen of the Adriatic.

The fact that Venice was in a position to make such a claim sprang from her historical role as capital (though technically a republic) of an empire that had at one time embraced much of the littoral of the north-eastern Mediterranean – what today is Yugoslavia, Greece, Cyprus and Crete – and there is more than a hint of the Orient in the fabric of St Mark's itself. It is also significant that there is no Bishop or even Archbishop of Venice as such, but a Patriarch, on the lines of Antioch and Constantinople. There has always been a touch of the exotic in things Venetian, and her music has been no exception. As Venice declined it seemed that her ceremonial grew more complex and more magnificent, and since St Mark's was the Doge's chapel, few Venetian institutions – and there were many of them – were able to compete with its splendour. It had two organs and two choir lofts, offering the physical possibility of elaborate antiphonal effects, which the resident musicians were not slow to exploit. St Mark's employed both choirmasters and organists, so that instead of having to choose between a good choir trainer and a brilliant organist in charge of music, the authorities were able to have both. Some of the greatest organists of their day were drawn to St Mark's – Annibale Padovano, Claudio Merulo, Andrea and Giovanni Gabrieli and Gioseffo Guami.

Adrian Willaert became *maestro di cappella* relatively early in the sixteenth century – in 1527 – and taught both his immediate predecessor, Cipriano de Rore, and his successor, Gioseffo Zarlino, as well as such men as Andrea Gabrieli and Nicolò Valentino. As is evident from the regularity with which names appear, musically there was no hard-and-fast division between organists and choirmasters, except of course in the exercise of their offices. Almost all of them wrote music of one sort or another, and Willaert produced work in nearly every genre – Masses and motets, French *chansons* and Italian madrigals, as well as distinguished instrumental music. Giovanni Gabrieli, possibly a better composer than organist, took some important steps towards the Baroque, as we shall see; and it is no exaggeration to say that if these musicians were not wholly inspired by the conditions and atmosphere at St Mark's, then they were undoubtedly greatly facilitated by them.

Of course Venice was by no means alone in its development of music at this time. Rome, Florence, Ferrara, Mantua and Milan all had their musical establishments, but it was Venice that gave the lead. One of the most flamboyant and therefore typically Venetian developments, however, was that of the *ricercar* which, in its early days, was a rather short piece of music consisting largely of running passages of notes and block chords. Examples of this can be seen in the books of lute music printed in Venice in 1507 and 1508 by Ottaviano dei Petrucci. There are also, incidentally, sets of dances in these books that anticipate the French suites of Bach. From the point of view of the immediate development of instrumental technique in Venice, however, the *ricercar* was taken up by the organists, since the block chords could be well sustained on the organ, while the running notes became ever more florid. In the hands of Andrea Gabrieli it might be a fantasia, or with Claudio Merulo a toccata (from *toccare*, meaning to touch). With such rapid flights of notes, it seems as if the fingers simply skim the keys in their passage. It is a style supremely suited to the organ, and one that retains its attraction for both composers and performers today.

This development was not only a Venetian speciality: a Roman school of keyboard music existed, too, and there was also a tradition by which alternate stanzas of Gregorian hymns were sung by the choir and then played on the organ, often with considerable embroidery of the tune in the organ stanzas. In Venice the scope for experiment seemed endless. Andrea Gabrieli, Adrian Willaert and Giovanni Gabrieli all wrote *ricercari*, and the last of these at times came very near to producing a fugue as his examples became more polyphonic. Even more interesting is his *sonata pian'e forte*, which is one of the earliest works to indicate soft and loud (*piano* and *forte*), a means of varying sound that we tend to take for granted, but of which most people then were unaware, so far as we can tell.

Sonata in this context simply means a composition meant to be 'sounded' by instruments rather than voices. The forces required are two four-part ensembles, in this case the three lower voices of each choir being taken by trombones, and the top lines being taken by a cornett and a *violino*, which was more like a viola than a violin as we know it. As yet instrumentation – the assignment of roles to instruments for their specific tonal qualities – was in its infancy, and the use of the word 'choir' deliberately emphasizes the fact that in concept there was little or no difference in the way a composer saw the deployment of his forces, be they vocal or instrumental. This is further demonstrated by the way the music was handled. Gabrieli used the two choirs of instruments antiphonally for contrast, and then combined them for other effects – methods which also applied to vocal choral technique. His *Jubilate Deo*, printed in 1597, used instruments and voices in this way, and two other pieces, probably written after 1600, took the possibilities even further. *Suscipe clementissime*, for example, used a six-part chorus that was contrasted with a choir of six trombones; the impressive *In ecclesiis*, probably his most ambitious and brilliant composition in this style, has two four-part choruses with, in addition, a group of four soloists, an organ, and an instrumental ensemble consisting of violas, cornetts and trombones. By this time, however, there was a move towards making

ABOVE The Sistine Chapel in Rome, whose choir and musical tradition set the pattern for the whole of Catholic Christendom for centuries.

RIGHT An Italian Renaissance positive organ in the classical style, the base decorated with scenes from the Bible; the arms at the top on either side are those of the Roveres, the family of Julius II, the Renaissance Pope.

a distinction between the way in which solo and choral parts were written and, perhaps more significantly, between the instrumental and the vocal writing.

Towards the Baroque

Before turning to the Baroque we must take into account certain other factors, and since Church music was the last subject dealt with, it makes a convenient point of departure. As we saw, the Reformation brought about a great division in the sphere of Church music, though to assume that the Protestants all went one way and the Catholics another is misleading. In Protestant Germany, for example, Luther certainly gave great emphasis to the chorale, but at the same time he retained a large amount of the existing liturgy. In England, on the other hand, the break was much more decisive, although this did not prevent the authorities from giving a monopoly of music-printing to William Byrd and Thomas Tallis. Both wrote for the new liturgy, but their music for the Catholic rite and Latin texts is by far the most inspired of their Church music. Byrd was in any case known to be a Catholic, and was tolerated as such.

If we turn to the Catholic Church and the deliberations of the Council of Trent, which between 1545 and 1563 attempted to put the Church's house in order in the light of the threat from the Reformation, the outcome there – as far as music was concerned – was a marked attempt at restraining the more extreme practices that had crept in, in response to criticism from outside the Church and from within. Effectively it made Palestrina's style of composition virtually the model for post-Tridentine Catholic Church music. The legend that it was Palestrina who, single-handed, preserved polyphony by his composition of the *Pope Marcellus Mass* is attractive, but is not supported by facts. What is certainly more likely is that the 1561 setting of the special prayers that were sung during the sittings of the council by Jacobus de Kerle (*c.*1532–91) demonstrated to the clerics that it was possible to write polyphonic music that was spiritual in content, sober in tone, and above all conducive to devotion.

There were other forces at work, however, over which the Church no longer had any control. Once the medieval world disintegrated, as far as the Church's hold was concerned, not only did the difference in Europe between north and south become apparent, but the whole emphasis in the balance between sacred and secular was irrevocably altered. It was henceforth possible for a composer to think of a career parallel to, or even outside of, the ecclesiastical world, and indeed the forms of Mass, motet and madrigal (though largely secular in context) reached the peak of their development in about 1600, after which they declined in importance, certainly in their seminal influence on the development of the main stream of Western music. There were of course enormous masterpieces still to come, such as Bach's B minor Mass, and Beethoven's *Missa solemnis*, but the former

ABOVE The English composer Thomas Tallis (*c.* 1505–85), from a series of engravings by Vandergucht and Haym.

LEFT A detail from *David in the Temple* by Lastman, in the Herzog Anton Ulrich Museum, Brunswick. The singers are accompanied by lute, viol, *rauschpfeife* and trombone, violin and tambourine with jingles.

71

may be seen as a delayed Indian summer, and the latter is only incidentally, as it were, religious music.

The emphasis on instrumental music grew in the late sixteenth century. Some compositions were, of course, inspired by vocal models, as in Venice, but there was an increasing demand for music for dancing and for courtly entertainments. Improvization continued to play an important role in the sort of instrumental music produced, but a significant spur to it now was the technique of the variation as a means of giving extended form to compositions. More than this, however, the music itself was seen as being capable of expressing emotions or feelings on its own, without having to rely on words to convey meaning; it was able to transcend words. A growing awareness of the expressiveness of the solo voice meant that increasingly it was accompanied only by instruments rather than forming part of a group. This was, perhaps, an inevitable consequence of the Renaissance and the new consciousness of man's nature and role in the world, but in it we can see already the seeds which would produce new forms of music in the Baroque period.

Venice was admirably suited for the encouragement of these tendencies, and indeed there were elements in the Venetian character that positively demanded it, and drew from composers the vivid, extrovert expression that impelled so much of their music. Without the Venetian dimension, it is conceivable that opera would have remained an aristocratic and private entertainment, as it was in Rome, for considerably longer than it did, and it is highly significant that the first public opera house opened in Venice. Girolamo Parabosco, writing in the middle of the sixteenth century, declared: 'Those Venetians are the sort of people who climb walls, break down doors and swim across canals in their haste to reach the places where any tragedy or comedy is being performed'; and it was Palladio's declared intent that he wished to give Venice the most beautiful church in the world, and with it a theatre worthy of the gods. This pronounced accent in favour of drama and theatre, when allied to a love of music as a necessary background to and essential part of almost every religious and secular ceremony, created a climate in Venice that encouraged the Baroque style in music.

In all this there is one figure who particularly stands out, and although his significance as a composer puts him in the next chapter, since he was born well within the sixteenth century, he must be introduced here. Claudio Monteverdi (1567–1643) was born at Cremona, and taught by the *maestro di cappella* at the cathedral there, Marc' Antonio Ingegneri (*c.* 1547–92). In 1590 Monteverdi joined the musical staff of Vincenzo Gonzaga, Duke of Mantua. Earlier that year he had produced his second book of madrigals; the first had been published in 1587, and the third was to appear in 1592. In 1602 Monteverdi became *maestro* of the duke's chapel, but he was poorly paid and overworked, his wife died when he was forty, and as a result he was not particularly happy during his time at Mantua. The fourth

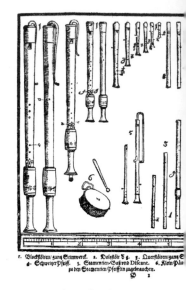

A woodcut showing a complete family of recorders from giant bass upwards, together with members of the flute family and a pipe and tabor, from Michael Praetorius' *Syntagma Musicum* of 1619.

A page from Giovanni Guidetti's *Directorium chori*, published in Rome in 1582. This book was the first to appear with all the chants after the reforming Council of Trent, and contained the basic elements for singing the Office or services of the Church.

and fifth books of madrigals appeared in 1603 and 1605, and though Monteverdi remained at Mantua until the death of the duke, it was only really when he went to Venice, where he spent the last thirty years of his life and became a priest in 1632, that he found lasting happiness and a sense of fulfilment.

The following quotations vividly indicate the change that had taken place not only in Monteverdi's own music, but in music generally. In response to criticism of his works, Monteverdi ended the preface to his fifth book of madrigals with the words: 'The modern composer builds on the foundations of truth'; in 1607 his brother Giulio Cesare wrote: 'My brother's intention has been to make the words the mistress of the music, and not the slave.' This was

The Glory of the Angels by
Ludovico Carracci
(1555–1619) in the
Church of San Paolo,
Bologna.

This late sixteenth-century Italian spinet in the Horniman Museum, London, is notable for its small size, emphasizing the reduced scope of the instrument by comparison with the harpsichord.

a result of the Renaissance and its concern with classical antiquity, for it was really an attempt to produce what was firmly believed to be the practice of the Greeks. Possibly the suggestion originated from a Roman, Girolamo Mei, but it was elaborated in Florence among a group of literary and musical figures known as the Camerata. The theory of monody was expressed by Vincenzo Galilei (c.1520–91), the father of the astronomer. Galilei wrote that the right way to set words was to employ a solo voice, for only in this way could one achieve the perfect fusion of melody and rhythm proper to the musical expression of any given phrase or sentence. Unfortunately his own setting of some verses from Dante's *Inferno* for tenor solo and viols has been lost, so we do not know how well he was able to put the theory into practice, but two composers who were both singers – Jacopo Peri (1561–1633) and Giulio Caccini (c.1546–1618) – took up the theory but prevented it from predominating, and so produced music that was eminently vocal. It soon caught on and in the early years of the seventeenth century influenced almost every kind of music, both secular and sacred. In 1600 Peri and Caccini collaborated on a setting of Ottavio Rinuccini's *Euridice* for the celebration of the wedding of Marie de' Medici to Henri IV of France, and it was performed publicly in Florence that year. Its success encouraged

ABOVE The title page of
Parthenia, London 1611,
which was the first
engraved collection of
music for keyboard
instruments. It included
works by John Bull,
William Byrd and
Orlando Gibbons.

LEFT A detail from the
right hand panel of
Hieronymus Bosch's
triptych *The Garden of
Earthly Delights*, in the
Prado, Madrid, in which
musical instruments
become part of the
physical tortures of the
damned.

each of the composers to produce his own version, which they did the
following year.

It was this attention to the text, as well as the monodic approach,
that eventually gave rise to the distinction in opera between recitative
and aria, and it was the innate musicianship of Peri and Caccini that
made them realize that long passages of unrelieved monody, such as
Galilei would have envisaged, would ultimately be boring for the
listener, no matter how novel it might seem at first. Consequently
they broke into the monody with short choral refrains or more
tuneful sections known as *arioso* passages. The result of this was
recitative, pure and simple, in which the narrative or plot was usually
developed, and arias and choruses, in which the singers commented
on the action, or expressed the emotion inspired by it. In this way,
then, the stage was set for the advance of Baroque music, and opera in
particular.

3. Baroque

The meaning of Baroque

The word Baroque was borrowed by music historians from the realm of art and architecture, where its original definition was somewhat pejorative: it meant 'strange' or even 'absurd'. Attempts to trace the etymology to the Portuguese *barroco* (a rough or irregular pearl) have not won a great deal of support. Whatever the precise derivation of the word, in music the Baroque period is thought to cover the century and a half from 1600 to 1750. It is evident from the previous chapter, however, that important changes had already taken place in music before 1600, and further changes were to occur well before 1750. There were also important historical events, such as the Thirty Years' War (1618–48) in Germany, the Fronde in France (1648–53), and the Civil War and Commonwealth period in England (1642–60) which caused great upheavals in artistic life.

The three chief characteristics of Baroque music, seen in the broadest possible terms, were expression, articulation and effect. These qualities had not been absent before, of course, but particular emphasis was placed on them during this period. Music that was concerned with all three – or even any one – of these characteristics may, however, seem rather unsatisfying and disappointing to us, as if the means of expression for which the Baroque composers were searching simply did not exist, much as one feels that Beethoven in his Ninth Symphony found the means at his disposal inadequate for what he wanted to communicate. The introduction of the name of a Romantic composer must not cloud the issue as far as expression itself is concerned, for Baroque composers had not yet reached the Romantic concern with being able to express the feelings of the artist as an individual. They were mostly concerned only with representing emotions and affections, but the way in which they did this – the articulation – was controlled by very precise and detailed means. This alone shows that the term Baroque in music has nothing of the haphazard or irregular in it as far as the theory is concerned. Everything is calculated for its ultimate effect, and the handling, or

Of all the instruments, perhaps the organ best conveys the enormous range of Baroque music, especially when allied so closely to the splendours of a Baroque church interior.

79

even manipulation, of the individual elements to achieve the ultimate effect probably most nearly touches the application of the term Baroque in painting, sculpture and architecture.

Composers were to a greater or lesser degree aware of all this. For example, in 1605 Monteverdi distinguished between what he called his *prima prattica* or first method, and his *seconda prattica*. His first method referred to the vocal polyphony that had come from the Netherlands to Venice and which had been seen supremely in the work of Willaert; his second, however, signified what Cipriano de Rore, Marenzio and he himself were doing, and in essence meant that whereas, before, music had dominated the text, now the reverse was true. Others used such definitions as *stile antico* and *stile moderno*, or *stylus gravis* and *stylus luxurians*. As the seventeenth century progressed, and such classifications proliferated, the differences between the old and the new became less marked; people realized that the distinction was in fact threefold, and by this time lay not so much in the contrast with the past, but in whether or not the music was intended for the Church, the theatre or the chamber.

Monteverdi and the rise of opera

Monteverdi's output illustrates these three divisions. Despite his long tenure of office at St Mark's, and having taken holy orders after the death of his wife, there is little to suggest that he was a specially devoted composer of religious music. The appeal of such a relatively small work as his setting of *Beatus vir* (Psalm 112), with its dancing figures, or even the monumental *Vespers* of 1610, lies more in the appeal of the works as absolute music than for anything else, let alone as devotional music. There are plenty of examples of chamber music – though not perhaps in the usual, later sense of the term – in books seven and eight of the madrigals (1619 and 1638), and as a composer of opera Monteverdi occupies a special place in the history of Western music. To all his work, however, Monteverdi brought his understanding of the joys and sorrows of human existence, and it is that element that gives it its unity, over and above purely technical considerations.

Monteverdi wrote more than twelve operas, but only three of them survive in anything like complete form. The first, *Orfeo*, was performed in 1607 and published in 1609, while the other two, *Il ritorno d'Ulisse in patria* (1641) and *L'incoronazione di Poppea* (1642) are late works that have come down to us in manuscript. Of a fourth opera, *Arianna*, very little now exists; a fragment, the heroine's haunting lament, has survived in an arrangement for five voices in Monteverdi's sixth book of madrigals, and also in a religious version. The differences between the first and two last operas are artificially exaggerated, of course, by the fact that no intervening works remain.

In *Orfeo*, Monteverdi showed that he had worked hard at mastering the new recitative as it then existed, and he used it to great effect. He also introduced choruses, which were used quite extensively in Rome, where the resources of private patrons of the opera were such that they could well afford them. When opera became public and commercial in Venice after 1637, it was simply not possible to provide lavish costumes and scenery, with star singers, as well as a full orchestra and chorus, and the last two items suffered severely as a result. Also for commercial reasons, the orchestral colour initiated in *Orfeo* never developed in Venetian opera to any great extent. Nevertheless one of the tendencies of Baroque composers was their readiness to write music for a specific medium, such as the solo voice or a particular instrument, rather than music that might be performed by almost any combination or permutation of voices and instruments. As we shall see, it was this disposition, combined with the rise of the Italian violin school, that produced such momentous results for later generations across the whole spectrum of concerted music. A great deal of the controversy over the orchestration of Monteverdi's operas arises not from any doubt that there was a varied range of texture, but what exactly might be included in that texture.

One school of thought assumes that if we know that a certain

number of instrumentalists were on the payroll of any given establishment, then as likely as not they would be employed when an opera was performed. Some critics are more cautious, preferring to base their conclusions on what we know was definitely the practice. The sources for such information are relatively scant, and the truth probably lies somewhere between the two; what is certain is that the rise of opera made more established orchestral bodies a necessity if the performance was to be repeated in another city. Once this happened, such orchestras became a regular feature of royal and princely households. Since there already tended to be a body of wind players on hand, as well as the more military trumpets and drums used for state occasions, the way was opened up for the orchestra to become an entity in its own right, and the Renaissance tendency to develop complete families of the same instrument came full circle as those families were now brought back together to form, eventually, the modern orchestra.

Perhaps the most important single development in the field of musical instruments was the emergence of the violin. The lives of the three great makers span almost 150 years: they are Niccolò Amati (1596–1684), Antonio Stradivari (1644–1737) and Giuseppe Bartolomeo Guarneri (1698–1744). As they gradually refined the instrument they achieved an infinitely brighter tone, and this resulted in an increase in the total number of string players in a large ensemble simply to redress the tonal balance, a pattern of expansion which continued at St Mark's throughout the seventeeth century. Towards the end of the century Legrenzi, the *maestro di cappella* at St Mark's, undertook a revision of the instrumental forces by reducing the number of upper strings, precisely because the tone of the violin had been developed to such an extent. In order to gauge the brilliance of the violin's tonal effect in the seventeenth century, we must imagine the reaction of a person of that time on hearing its hard, bright focus in contrast to the soft tonal quality of the viol. Such incision responded to and further encouraged the Baroque composers' search for articulation and expression. When the third characteristic of Baroque music – effect – is recalled, one sees what an important impetus was given to the development of instrumental music as a medium in its own right at this time.

A comparable development in vocal music, as we have seen, was the recitative, and an important factor in this was the thorough bass or *basso continuo*. Here the composer wrote out the melody or voice part in full but only the bass line for the accompaniment, with a series of figures looking rather like fractions to represent the chords that were to be played by the continuo or supporting instrument – often a keyboard instrument such as a harpsichord or organ, or possibly a lute. There would also be a sustaining instrument such as a bass gamba, or later a cello or bassoon. Over this bass or foundation, the keyboard or lute performer would fill in an accompaniment, using the figures as a guide to the harmonies to be used. This is known as

Antonio Stradivari (1644–1737) is best known as a maker of violins, but he also made excellent guitars like this one with five double string-courses. Made at Cremona in 1688, it is now in the Hill Collection at the Ashmolean Museum, Oxford.

realizing a figured bass, and the actual notes played are left entirely to the skill and imagination of the performer. Another form of bass encountered at this time was the *basso ostinato*, or 'insistent' bass, in which the same phrase was repeated several times. Monteverdi used this in his *Beatus vir* referred to earlier, and although it was by no means as important as the *basso continuo*, it played a considerable part later on in the development of some forms of instrumental music – such as the passacaglia and the chaconne. *Basso continuo*, on the other hand, was of fundamental importance as the seventeenth century progressed, for through it can be traced the route taken by music as it went from counterpoint to harmony, or from a conception of music that was linear and melodic to one that was chordal and harmonic. After about the middle of the eighteenth century, when the whole harmonic system was so well established that it no longer needed the help of the *basso continuo*, it withered away.

If we take a final look at Monteverdi's two last operas, we find a world full of contrasts, with comic scenes to emphasize the passionate ones, a rich variety of human emotion, and a combination of recitative and *arioso* (in which there is no developed melody but the regularity of the rhythm indicates that it is different from the recitative). We see the emergence of the aria in, for example, the lullaby sung by Arnalta in *L'incoronazione di Poppea*. With the arrival of the aria, the *arioso* tended to fade, for the aria allowed the singer to demonstrate his or her talent to the full, and it was also a means of encapsulating a situation in dramatic terms. With this development the establishment of opera as it became known to the world was well on the way. Abuses inevitably crept in, and at times the standing of opera was brought into serious disrepute; nevertheless, at its best it is capable of being one of the most stimulating of all musical forms.

New forms in instrumental music

The exciting phenomenon of Italian opera could easily overshadow some other important developments, especially in the field of instrumental music, but opera does not provide a true picture of activity in the instrumental field, since it was affected by specific factors: the forces available to operatic composers were conditioned primarily by financial considerations; moreover the approach of composers to operas tended to be rather fluid, and there was no conception of a 'definitive' version, so that a performance given in one city might be considerably altered when it appeared elsewhere.

In Church and chamber music, of which much was published, we can detect the origins of two important forms in the future of music – concerto and sonata. Many of these were first heard in churches, where they were known as *sonate da chiesa*, and in Venice they became a feature that people flocked from all over Europe to hear. In Venice four female orphanages made music a speciality, and the fact that the whole ensemble usually consisted of girls proved to be an added

Arcangelo Corelli
(1653–1713), a portrait
after a half-length
painting by Hugh
Howard *c.* 1699.

attraction. The music of Giovanni Gabrieli provides us with examples of both the sonata and the concerto; he was in fact one of the earliest composers to make use of the word concerto. In terms of instrumental sonorities the essential feature of the concerto was contrast, a characteristic that it still retains. The contrast might be between different groups of instruments, or the same instruments used in contrasting groups, and joining together at certain points in the music.

One of the most popular concerto forms to emerge was that known as the *concerto grosso*, essentially a contrast between a small, soloistic

ABOVE Alessandro
Scarlatti (1660–1725), as
depicted by an
anonymous artist in a
portrait in the museum at
Bologna.

RIGHT Georg Philipp
Telemann (1681–1767) in
an etching by Preissler
(1750) of Ludwig Michael
Schneider's portrait.

group of strings and continuo and the rest of the group. In Italy Arcangelo Corelli (1653–1713) was perhaps the most important exponent of the form, though Alessandro Stradella (1644–82), Giuseppe Torelli (1658–1709) and Tomaso Albinoni (1671–1750) all made important contributions to it. It was a form that gained a following abroad, and Jean-Marie Leclair (1697–1764) in France, Georg Philipp Telemann (1681–1767) in Germany and William Boyce (1710–79) and George Frideric Handel in England all took it up. Some of Handel's most popular music is contained in his *concerti grossi*. Another exponent was Francesco Geminiani (*c*.1680–1762), who had studied with both Corelli and Alessandro Scarlatti (1660–1725), but was dismissed from the post he held in Naples because the players were unable to follow his changes of tempo and use of *rubato* (the holding up of the music inside a phrase for effect), which was considered excessive.

This fascination with contrasts and textures was to inspire much of Italian instrumental music for the rest of the seventeenth century and much of the eighteenth. It can be seen in music as early as the organ music of Girolamo Frescobaldi (1583–1643), though by and large Italian organ-playing did not compare well with that of France and Germany at this time. In other fields, however, the Italians produced important developments. Bologna, for example, had an excellent school of trumpet-playing, and composers such as Giacomo Perti (1661–1756), Maurizio Cazzati (*c*.1620–77) and Torelli wrote sonatas and concertos for the instrument that greatly enriched its repertoire. Albinoni in Venice wrote beautiful oboe concertos, and Vivaldi seemed to delight in endless exploration of tonal and textural possibilities, and wrote concertos for many different instruments. Of course both Albinoni and Vivaldi wrote trio sonatas as well, which were much more intimate works, and an almost obligatory stage for any composer to pass through in his development, but Vivaldi's importance in particular lies in his contribution to the form of the concerto.

Antonio Vivaldi (1678–1741) was a priest, but managed to have a career as composer, impresario, teacher and virtuoso violinist at the same time. In fact it was as a violinist that he was first known in his native city of Venice. Of course he did not establish the Italian violin school. Corelli, and even Torelli, made earlier and important contributions, and Tartini was later to make further experiments in an attempt to solve technical problems, but Vivaldi's restless exploitation of the potential of both his own instrument and others, as well as the fascination with textures that he displayed, give him a special place in the development of the concerto. Not all his music is of a consistently high standard, though, and much of his operatic music is perfunctory, to say the least.

The quality of operatic music generally, after Monteverdi, has been rather deplored so far in this book, and it is true to say that once Monteverdi and his immediate successors Francesco Cavalli (1602–76) and Pietro Cesti (1623–69) were left behind, musical integrity quickly departed. Nevertheless the opera house gave to musical posterity an important legacy in the overtures that were played there. In Rome one of the earliest opera composers was Stefano Landi (*c*.1590–*c*.1655), and his *Sant' Alessio* is an important landmark from several points of view. In this context it is particularly the prelude to the first act, or *sinfonia* – a word of Greek derivation that originally meant simply 'sounding together' – that is interesting. It opens with a slow chordal section, which is followed by a faster, polyphonic one, later developed into the French overture by Lully

RIGHT The only authentic likeness of the Venetian composer Antonio Vivaldi (1678–1741) is this caricature by Pier Leone Ghezzi dating from 1723 and now in the Vatican Library, Rome.

ABOVE Girolamo Frescobaldi (1583–1643), as depicted in a portrait in the Louvre Museum, Paris.

RIGHT An example of Vivaldi's musical handwriting from the allegro movement of the sixth concerto, volume eight of the Giordano Collection in the University Library, Turin.

and others. The two other *sinfonie* of Landi's opera are both in three sections, on the pattern of two fast sections on either side of a slow middle one. These look forward to the form that became known, in the hands of Alessandro Scarlatti, as the Italian overture, and which led ultimately to the development of the classical symphony, almost eclipsing the French overture on the way.

Brief reference was made earlier to the sonata and trio sonata, and before leaving Italian instrumental music we must take a closer look at the whole concept of the sonata. There is a very close parallel between the sonata and the *sinfonia* in that basically they both imply a sounding together of instruments. In fact the similarity is somewhat closer than this, since they both had their origins as purely instrumental passages in a primarily vocal piece of music. Whereas the *sinfonia* has been identified closely with the opera, the sonata is traced back to the *canzona*, but *canzona* was such a vague term, especially in the early seventeenth century, that it is difficult to be more specific. In the case of the *sonata da chiesa*, one might well say

Hic fidibus, scriptis, claris hic magnus alumnis
... nemo fuit forte nec ...

Guiseppe Tartini
(1692–1770) in an
engraved portrait by
Carolus Calcinoto.

that it assimilated the *canzona*. What emerges after about 1660, however, is a distinction between the more serious *sonata da chiesa* and the *sonata da camera*, which was virtually a suite of dance movements.

The two terms were by no means mutually exclusive, for often church sonatas included dance movements, although not always indicated as such, and chamber sonatas might have movements that were not dance movements. Almost within a decade, however, both these kinds of sonata were being designated trio sonatas since they were written for two upper instruments and bass, the harmonies being filled out by the continuo, as we saw in the previous section.

This meant that although it was called a trio sonata, because it consisted essentially of three parts of music, it actually required four players, because the continuo consisted of both a keyboard and a bass instrument. By the end of the seventeenth century this had become an established form; Albinoni, for example, published a collection of trio sonatas as his *Opus I*, in 1694, and Vivaldi did the same in 1705. After the turn of the century, however, the solo sonata, for a solo instrument and continuo, became common, the solo instrument often being a violin or flute.

Obviously the popularity of sonata form sprang from the fact that it was a relatively easy essay in composition, and since it required few performers it had more likelihood of being played. But to say only that is grossly to underestimate the craftsmanship and talent of the composers involved. In one respect at least it corresponded directly to one of the three basic concerns of Baroque music, namely articulation, with expression close on its heels. It was also an admirable way of investigating the possibilities of the violin, and indeed marks its emergence as the chief voice among the instruments on the concert platform and in the opera house pit right up to the present time. It also symbolizes the way in which the instrumentalist had established himself as a virtuoso in his own right, and not merely as a subsidiary to the singer. More profoundly, perhaps, it denoted the completion of the process outlined at the outset of the Baroque period – that music no longer needed words to convey its meaning; it could exist independently.

The Italian influence in France

Italy has featured almost exclusively in our consideration of the development of seventeenth-century Western music simply because it was Italy that gave almost the whole of the rest of Europe its music, and set the pattern that other countries were to follow. But we shall now consider what happened when its influence went abroad, and because of the close ties that bound the two countries, we turn first to France.

Unlike Italy or Germany, which at this time were still only geographical conceptions as opposed to political realities, France was already a stable country, with a centralized monarchy. In fact for all but the first decade of the seventeenth century only two men ruled France – Louis XIII and Louis XIV, whose reigns together spanned 105 years. The history of French music of this time is therefore virtually the history of music at court. Naturally it was aristocratic music, but it also covered almost every aspect of daily life, for there were eight groups of musicians in permanent employment at court, supplying music for the royal chapel, chamber music for concerts on Sundays, concerts for eating, music for soirées and dancing – as well as specially mounted ballets and operas – and even music for hunting. This had its unfortunate side, however, in that if a composer could

The title page of the first violin part of Vivaldi's first published work, dating from 1705, which was a collection of trio sonatas dedicated to the Venetian nobleman Annibale Gambara.

gain the King's confidence, he could have almost total control over the careers of other composers, even to the extent of restricting the sort of music they wrote. In short, such concentration of activity made it possible for a kind of musical monopoly to be exercised in France.

Since so many musical influences came from Italy, if Italian styles were introduced and found favour, then Italian influence would predominate. This was encouraged by the fact that Louis XIII was not ten years old when he came to the throne in 1610, and his mother, the Italian Marie de Médicis (the French version of her name), acted as regent initially and leaned heavily on the advice of another Italian, Concino Concini. His baleful influence lasted only until 1617, however, when he was assassinated. The King later gave power to Cardinal Richelieu. A similar situation arose when Louis XIV came to the throne, at an even younger age than Louis XIII had been at his accession, but his mother, Anne of Austria, had the wisdom to follow the advice given by Richelieu on his deathbed the year before, and appoint another Italian, Cardinal Mazarin, as principal adviser. Mazarin naturally imported many Italian musicians, and even whole opera companies, but Italian opera did not appeal to the French; yet neither would they evolve a form of their own – at first, that is. In musical terms the dilemma can be summed up by the work of two composers: Marc-Antoine Charpentier (1634–1704) and Jean-Baptiste Lully (1632–87). When we learn that Lully was in fact an Italian (born Lulli) who only came to France at the age of ten, the matter becomes clearer.

It seems that Lully first captivated the young Louis XIV by his violin-playing, and was appointed to the special band of twenty-four violinists known as *Les Vingt-quatre Violons du Roi*. In 1656, however, he sought the King's permission – which was granted – to set up a smaller band of only sixteen violins known as *Les Petits Violons*, which he later expanded to twenty-one. When the smaller group became much better than the original, Lully became conductor of the King's Violins. Such single-mindedness marked Lully's career. Some time before, realizing that unless he was able to play the harpsichord and compose music he would never get very far, he took lessons and displayed such a talent for composition that he was asked to contribute music for a court ballet in 1653 organized by the poet Isaac de Benserade (1613–91) and entitled *La Nuit*. It was in this ballet that Louis XIV danced the part of the Sun King – *Le Roi Soleil* – so well that he kept the title for the rest of his life.

It was quite common practice for composers to share the work of providing music for the court ballets – the same thing happened in England. However, when Lully collaborated with Benserade again in 1658 on *Alcidiane*, he wrote all the music, and it was so successful that he determined never to share the honours again. He did, however, provide music for operas, and when Cavalli's *Serse* and *Ercole amante* were performed in 1660 and 1662 respectively, they both had music

RIGHT A member of the French king's band of violinists in an engraving of 1688. There were twenty-four members of the band in all, and their duty was to provide music for the wide variety of events that constituted the royal day.

LEFT Louis XIV danced the role of the Sun King – *Le Roi Soleil* – for a court ballet in 1653 and retained the title for the rest of his life.

LEFT Jean-Baptiste Lully (1632–87) in a portrait by Bonnart in the Windsor Collection of the Royal College of Music, London.

OVERLEAF A candlelit performance of Lully's opera *Alceste* given in the Marble Courtyard at Versailles in June 1676.

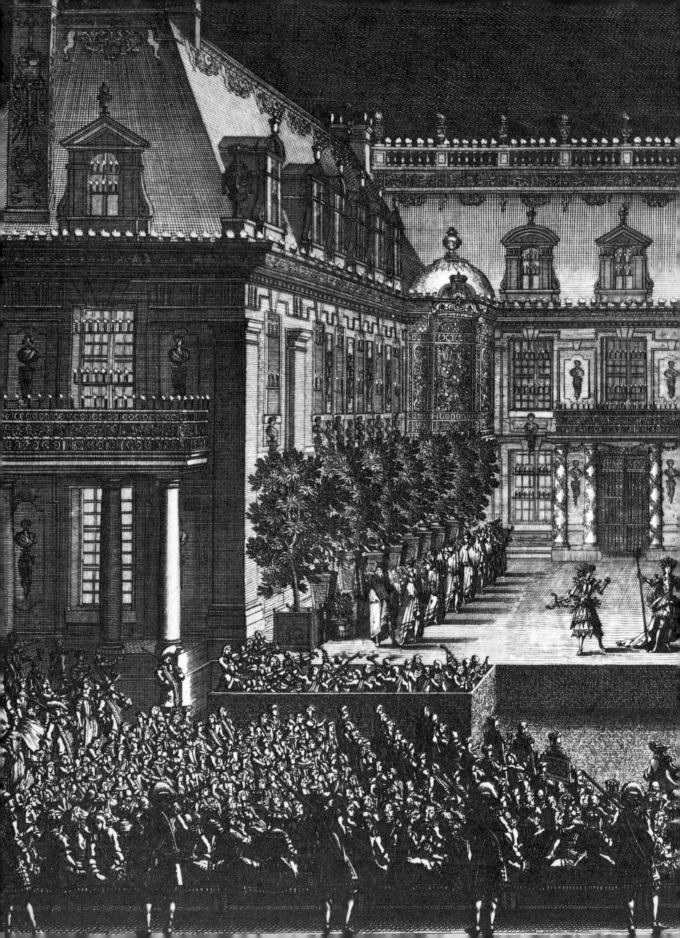

by Lully. Undoubtedly Lully took the opportunity to study the operas themselves, and though he had hitherto been dismissive of French attempts at opera, such as those of the librettist Pierre Perrin (*c*.1620–75) and the composer Robert Cambert (*c*.1628–77), the success of their *Pomone* in 1671, coupled with the founding of the Académie Royale de l'Opéra and the granting of a royal privilege to Perrin, spurred Lully to take action. He used all his influence with the King, and had the privilege taken away from Perrin, who died three years later in misery. Cambert went to England and entered the service of Charles II, and was subsequently assassinated in mysterious circumstances. Success did not improve Lully. In 1673, at his instigation, no theatre was allowed to employ more than two voices and six violins. In 1684, no opera might be performed without his permission. All one can say is that such dedicated ambition resulted in the creation, by Lully, of a truly French opera that lasted for more than a century. He died, it is said, as a result of an abscess caused by striking his foot with his baton while conducting a *Te Deum*.

Perhaps it had taken a foreigner – and an Italian at that – to decide what kind of vocal music best suited the French, and then serve it up to them. Having discovered the formula, Lully made certain that nothing was allowed to intrude, even to the extent of ensuring that certain young composers were prevented from going to Italy to study. It was therefore highly ironical that one who had gone to Italy to study with Carissimi – Marc-Antoine Charpentier – returned to France in about 1650 to find doors closed to him because he, a Frenchman, had returned with a style that was influenced by Italy, whereas an Italian held sway in Paris and dictated what was French music and what was not. For years Charpentier waited in the wings, and it was only after Lully's death, when Charpentier himself was over sixty, that he was appointed master of music at Ste Chapelle in Paris in 1698. By then Charpentier's potential development as an operatic composer had been well and truly stifled, and he devoted himself to religious music in the grand manner.

Style did change, however, and the direction it took can be seen in the work of two composers of the next generation: Couperin ('*Le Grand*') and Rameau. François Couperin was born in 1668, and although only eleven when his father died, he succeeded him as organist of the church of St Gervais in Paris. In 1693 he became organist of the chapel at Versailles. Today he is most remembered for his harpsichord music, and the fact that Bach copied some of it for himself, and that the two men were correspondents, is eloquent testimony to its qualities. In addition to playing the harpsichord and organ, Couperin also wrote Church music and directed the court chamber concerts on Sunday afternoons. He did not, however, compose any ballets or operas. There are several explanations for this. Louis XIV did not end his reign as he had begun it, and an air of increasing melancholy and piety hung over the court during the last

To celebrate the marriage of the French Dauphin to Maria Teresa of Spain in 1745, Rameau wrote a comedy ballet *La Princesse de Navarre* to Voltaire's text, which was staged in the riding school at Versailles.

LEFT Pipe and tabor, trumpet, harp and psaltery are used to illustrate literally the words of Psalm Eighty-one in King Henry VIII's Psalter in the British Museum.

Xultate Deo adiutori nostro:
iubilate Deo Iacob
Sumite pfalmum: & date tympanum
pfalterium iocundum cum cythara.

ABOVE Bathing to the sound of music in an enclosed garden which had its origin in the Garden of Eden, but is totally secularized as a Garden of Love in this illustration from a manuscript in the Biblioteca Estense, Modena, Italy.

RIGHT A painting by the unidentified artist known as the Master of the Female Half-Lengths, showing music dating from the early sixteenth century verified as being Claudin de Sermisy's *Jouyssance vous donneray*. The flute probably doubles the voice, and the lute plays the under parts.

twenty or so years of his reign. Couperin himself had always had a rather delicate constitution, and would not have had the stamina required of an opera composer; perhaps in any case he simply never had the inclination, and found fulfilment in what he already did.

As an indication of what might have been in store for Couperin, one has only to consider the fate of Jean-Philippe Rameau (1683–1764), who in 1733 – the year of Couperin's death – produced his first opera *Hippolyte et Aricie* when he was already fifty years old. He was decried as a traitor to Lully, and even when he stated in his preface to *Les Indes galantes* of 1735 that he had taken Lully as a model, this did not seem to reassure his critics. It is ironical – and the history of music is full of such ironies – that when, in 1752, a war (the *guerre des bouffons*) broke out over the relative merits of French and Italian music, more or less the same people who had condemned Rameau for betraying Lully now held him up as the most eminent French composer – in the tradition of Lully – in the face of those led by Rousseau, who supported Italian music. Rameau was an intellectual, a theorist, and his *Treatise on Harmony*, published more than ten years before he ventured on to the operatic stage, indicates where his interest chiefly lay. It is highly significant that Debussy should have looked back to Rameau and regretted that the French tradition he represented had been deflected from its path, and that the way back had been so long and painful. For Debussy, Rameau was the epitome of French musical genius.

England

France made its influence felt in England at the restoration of the monarchy in 1660, when Charles II, who had spent his exile there, returned with such a love of things French that he had a band of violins obviously modelled on that of the French court. This went hand in hand with a distaste for what he felt were the outdated survivals of English music. In fact the Commonwealth had not created such a break in English musical traditions as has often been suggested. Naturally the rift was most pronounced in Church music, and it seriously delayed the start of English opera, but considerably more secular and private music-making went on during the Commonwealth period than has usually been accredited. England was generally some way behind continental developments at the best of times, and there had been no new generation of composers to take over when the great Elizabethan and Jacobean composers disappeared, but on Charles II's restoration, the time slip was indeed pronounced, and was exaggerated by the Commonwealth interval and the King's contact with French developments.

Few people were more aware of this than the only English composer of international stature at the time, Henry Purcell (1659–95). As he wrote in his preface to *Dioclesian* in 1690:

Musick is yet but in its Nonage, a forward Child which gives hope of what it may be hereafter in England . . . 'Tis now learning Italian, which is its best Master, and studying a little of the French Air, to give it somewhat more of Gayety and Fashion. Thus being further from the Sun, we are of later growth than our Neighbour Countries, and must be content to shake off our Barbarity by degrees.

Purcell's own work bears this out. Some of his fantasias for strings, written when he was twenty or so, may well have seemed to smack of 'Barbarity' to Charles II, but two years later Purcell's trio sonatas indicated that he had certainly been 'learning Italian'. This first set of sonatas is more in the Church rather than the chamber tradition, but this is readily explained by the English situation and the fact that Purcell was the son and nephew of Church musicians. He himself was a chorister and organist, and succeeded Blow as organist of Westminster Abbey, though Blow had to return after Purcell's premature death.

Purcell's Church music contains the same kind of mixture as his chamber music, namely the survival of traditional forms in his 'full' anthems – though they were no less expressive or accomplished for that – and the Baroque tendencies of his newer 'verse' anthems, which also reflect the problem of reconstituting and equipping the choir of the royal chapel at the Restoration. Since there were few trained boys initially, the burden of the solo singing was put on the men, who sang the 'verses' or solo parts, and the boys joined in with a suitably short and joyful Hallelujah by way of chorus. Purcell himself was a distinguished counter-tenor and performer of his own solos, by all accounts, though the vocal ornamentation required for them, the abrupt changes of tempo and succession of different movements so typical of the Baroque, long remained foreign to the tradition of Anglican Church music. Nevertheless some of Purcell's most characteristic touches are to be found in the verse anthems, and for the Hallelujahs he wrote some stirring tunes, subsequently adapted for hymns.

Beyond the limited world of Church music, we can see clearly what Purcell might have achieved had he lived longer. The ode that he wrote for St Cecilia's Day in 1692 – *Hail, Bright Cecilia* – is in a class of its own, and the chorus 'Soul of the world' has an almost Handelian dimension. But it is for the opera *Dido and Aeneas* that he is, and deserves to be, chiefly remembered. Pre-dating the St Cecilia's Day ode by two or three years, it is on quite a different level from anything he wrote subsequently, and it is one of the great tragedies of English musical history that the last five or six years of Purcell's life were expended on providing music for plays that were little better than pantomimes. Despite the efforts of some native composers, it needed a Handel to take up the pen that Purcell laid down, but by the time he did so, English opera was dead, and for the next two hundred years Italian opera was to reign supreme.

OVERLEAF:
LEFT Orlando di Lasso with his musicians in the ducal chapel at Munich, *c*. 1580–90, from a miniature in the Staatsbibliothek, Munich.

CENTRE The violin by Antonio Stradivari known as the Messiah, made in Cremona in 1716 and now in the Ashmolean Museum, Oxford. Apart from its classical proportions and purity of line, it is significant because it has not been altered; it even has its original varnish.

ABOVE RIGHT The spinet in the Victoria and Albert Museum, London, usually known as Queen Elizabeth's Virginals. Probably a late sixteenth-century Italian instrument, it is made of cypress wood, and the panel on the left of the keyboard bears the coat-of-arms borne by English monarchs from Henry IV to Elizabeth I. On the right is the crowned falcon holding a sceptre, which was the device of Anne Boleyn, also used by her daughter, Elizabeth I.

BELOW RIGHT Detail from an allegory of Vanity by Leonhard Bramer (1596–1674), who was a follower of Rembrandt. Among the instruments depicted are a lute, two violins, a cittern, a flute and a bass viol.

Germany

Although the adjective German had always had a connotation with
which people identified, the region that is now Germany was similar
to Italy in that it consisted of a number of small states owing
allegiance to various rulers; what gave Germany the little geographical
and political unity that it had was its identification with the Holy
Roman Empire. From the fifteenth to the nineteenth century the
Emperor was a Habsburg who ruled from Vienna, and in theory was
elected by the representatives of the various autonomous territories
of the Empire. Even after the Reformation, when some of those
territories became Protestant, the Emperor remained a Catholic, and
continued to be 'elected'. It says a great deal for the system that it

A panel from a carved
wooden lectern (*c.* 1633)
in the Biecz Museum in
Poland. The town
musicians include a
singer, cornett player,
bass recorder player and
trumpeter.

A German engraving of 1698 by Christoph Weigel showing the workshop of a wind instrument maker, possibly the famous Denner.

continued to work for as long as it did, and indeed might have continued for much longer had not Napoleon decided to put an end to it, as he did to the Venetian Republic.

The implications of all this for music were that until the seventeenth century there was no great German music that we can at once point to as being essentially German, and there was no readily recognizable German musical identity. The composers who had hitherto achieved fame and were technically Germans, such as Heinrich Isaac or Jacob Handl (Gallus), for example, were really part of the Flemish school, and Hassler, born in Nuremberg, belonged to the Venetian tradition. Nevertheless there was something German in their predilection for a four-square tune, and for their way of accompanying it, which Luther approved of and indeed capitalized on, and which Bach also exploited. This tended to apply to the states that were Protestant more than to those that were Catholic, but even so it would be wrong to suppose that Luther only wanted chorales – he retained a large part of the liturgy, and firmly believed that music was a foretaste of heaven.

LEFT *Woman at the Virginals* (or spinet) by Jan Vermeer (1632–75), in the National Gallery, London. In the left foreground is a bass viol da gamba.

ABOVE George Frideric Handel (1685–1759) in an anonymous portrait thought to have been painted *c*. 1730, now in the National Portrait Gallery, London.

RIGHT Johann Sebastian Bach (1685–1750), painted as a young man by Johann Ernst Rentsch.

In one important field the Germans had already created a musical tradition, however, and that was organ music. German organs were developed sooner than elsewhere in Europe, and although many southern students were attracted to Venice, both for its proximity and its fame, there was an important northern centre in Amsterdam; Jan Pieterszoon Sweelinck (1562–1621) was organist at the Oude Kerk there, and produced a stream of brilliant organists who studied with him. He has been called the maker of German organists, but his talents were not restricted to organ tuition. He was an accomplished harpsichordist, and also composed instrumental pieces and secular part-songs. Scheidemann, Scheidt and Praetorius, three of his students, in turn produced pupils – Scheidemann taught Reinken, for example – who provided the link with those organists such as Pachelbel, Böhm and Buxtehude who were the celebrated names in J. S. Bach's youth.

Dietrich Buxtehude (c.1637–1707) was probably the greatest of

1. 2. Kleine Poschen / Geigen ein Octav höher. 3. Discant-Geig ein 4. Rechte Discant-Geig. 5. Tenor-Geig. 6 Bas-Geig de bracio. 7. 8. Schardeholtz.

n de Gamba. 4. Viol Baftarda. 5. Italianische Lyra de bracio.

them all, following his father-in-law Tunder (himself no mean talent) as organist of the Marienkirche in Lübeck, on the Baltic. Buxtehude's *Abendmusiken*, or concerts of evening music on the last five Sundays before Christmas, spread his fame throughout Germany and beyond. In 1699 Pachelbel dedicated his *Hexachordum Apollinis* to Buxtehude; in 1703 Mattheson and Handel travelled from Hamburg to visit him, and in 1705 Bach went 250 miles on foot to see him in Lübeck. As far as Handel and Bach were concerned, it must be admitted that a good part of the attraction was that as Buxtehude saw his career coming to an end he wished to find a successor, and one of the terms of the appointment was marriage with his daughter, just as he himself had married Tunder's daughter. His reputation in any case was such that he was able to draw such talented people to him, and they obviously felt that it would be an honour to succeed him. Buxtehude wrote religious vocal music as well, but his genius lay above all in his ability as an organist and composer for the organ, and his improvizations must have been marvellous to hear.

Before turning to J.S. Bach, since he belonged primarily to the great German organ tradition, we must consider some of the composers who emerged in the earlier part of the seventeenth century: a trio born in successive years were Schütz (1585–1672), Schein (1586–1630) and Scheidt (1587–1654). Of these the first was undoubtedly the greatest; in fact he was probably the greatest German musician of the century. Above all he was German, and remained so, despite the fact that he admired Italy enormously, and brought many ideas back with him from visits to Italy. He went to Venice twice, first as a pupil of Giovanni Gabrieli, and then during Monteverdi's time at St Mark's. But he displayed his German *individualismus* long before Germany was even a nation, and he had the 'German profundity' that Debussy so deplored when he looked back wistfully to Rameau, although the term is not applied pejoratively to Schütz, for with him it was rather a quality of mysticism. The fact that he was so generally loved by other musicians is a telling tribute to the nature of the man; in any generation the musicians of whom none of their colleagues will speak ill are rare beings.

In addition to his visits to Venice, Schütz went to Denmark at the invitation of the King, at a time when the Thirty Years' War made life in many parts of Germany very difficult; his principal occupation, however, from 1617 to the end of his life, was *Kapellmeister* to the Elector of Saxony in Dresden. His outlook was therefore aristocratic and formal, and more concerned with the solemn magnificence of court ceremonies than with more homely music of Germany. Schütz was an organist, but unfortunately he left no organ music, and in any case he showed no concern with chorale melodies. As far as we know he left no independent instrumental music either, though passages do, of course, occur in some of his accompanied vocal works. He is reputed to have written the first German opera, *Dafne*, as well as

LEFT The Galli-Bibiena family originated in Bologna, and, for more than a century from about 1670, no less than eight of them practised as architects and stage-designers throughout Europe. Here we see a Bibiena set for an opera on the story of Dido and Aeneas, at the point where the lovers are making their farewells.

BELOW A painting of Michel de la Barre and his colleagues in the National Gallery, London, which is attributed to Robert Tournières and thought to date from *c.* 1710. Three Hotteterre flutes and a viola da gamba are included in the picture.

ballets and stage works, but all that survives is his Church music.
Even so, from what we know of the man, and the way in which
he – unlike Bach – always chose texts exclusively from scripture or
the liturgy, it is probably right to regard his Church music as the
heart of his work. Emotional intensity is by no means lacking in it, but
it is essentially a controlled intensity, which only serves to heighten
its effect. It is customary to regard his settings of the Passion as
forerunners of Bach's, but even a cursory comparison reveals a totally
different conception. Bach gives us his insight into the message of the
Crucifixion, as something involving the whole of mankind, and he
paints it in suitably universal terms. With Schütz, however, it is a
quintessence, a distillation, of personal experience. There is no
comfort to be taken from our mutual responsibility as human beings :
each one of us stands as an individual, face to face with truth, and each
must make his individual response.

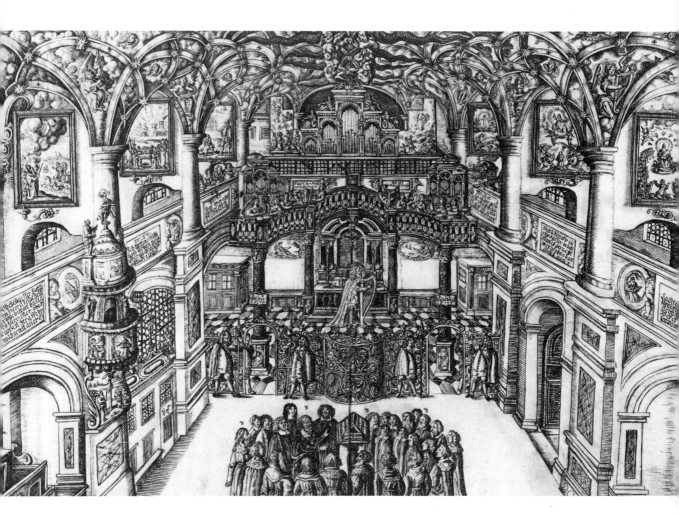

Rembrandt's portrait of
Heinrich Schütz
(1585–1672), in the
Corcoran Gallery of Art,
Washington.

The geniuses of Baroque music

We now turn to two more Germans, both born in 1685 – exactly a century after Schütz – who between them not only dominate their age, but are truly giants in the history of Western music. And to a certain extent they complement each other, for whereas Johann Sebastian Bach represents one aspect of musical genius, George Frideric Handel is a very different aspect of the same genius. It probably comes as some surprise, then, to learn that Bach, in his own day, enjoyed a reputation in Protestant Germany for virtuoso organ technique and as the composer of some rather academic pieces of music, but little else. Perhaps no one would be more surprised than Bach himself to return and find that he is now revered as a supreme composer, and a recognized exponent of almost all forms of late Baroque music except opera, though some of his arias are virtually operatic. He probably thought of himself first and foremost as a dedicated craftsman, and indeed in his laborious copying and arranging of the works of other composers – as a means of studying their compositions and getting to know them – there is a great deal that smacks of the solid musical tradition of his family and the part of Germany where they lived. But more than that, there was a doggedness and determination in Bach's own character that directed his whole career. One sees it at its most basic in the journeys on foot, not only to seek out Buxtehude, but also Handel (whom he narrowly missed meeting), and at its highest in the dedication of his genius to his ideals.

He served successively as organist at Arnstadt (1703–7) and Mühlhausen (1707–8), then as court organist and *Konzertmeister* at Weimar (1708–17), and as *Kapellmeister* to the Prince of Cöthen (1717–23). He made the conscious decision to resign from that post, and to go as cantor to St Thomas's School and then as Music Director to Leipzig, where he remained until his death in 1750. If we compare the sort of music normally expected from the *Kapellmeister* at this time – elegant, polished, international (though chiefly Italian) – and that produced by a cantor of the Lutheran Church, Bach's choice of the latter indicates that he believed that he could best fulfil himself in that direction. He had in any case assimilated all that he required from Italian and French music, and he wanted to dedicate himself to raising the standards and the status of both the music and the post of a Lutheran cantor.

Bach's religious music must surely be at the heart of his work – not only the monumental compositions such as the *St Matthew Passion*, the *St John Passion* and the B minor Mass, but the cantatas that he wrote for successive Sundays of the Church's year over a five-year period, and of which some 200 survive. Surely here was true dedication. There is enormous variation in style and content, ranging from the Christmas Oratorio (which is really a series of cantatas) to some that last no more than ten minutes. Amongst them are such sublime pieces as *Ich habe genug* (No. 82), with its famous solo aria

The frontispiece to
Bernhardi's *Geistreiches
Gesang-Buch* of 1676,
showing the interior of
the court chapel at
Dresden. Schütz can be
seen in the midst of the
singers around the music
stand, with his hand
raised.

and limpid oboe obbligato expressing a profound belief in the Christian afterlife, and *Vergnügte Ruh'* (No. 170), entirely for solo voice, which deals with much the same theme, though in even warmer melodic terms.

It would be foolish to pretend that all Bach's work is of an equal standard, and there are passages which even dedicated musicians will confess to finding rather boring. At times there can be a somewhat relentless quality in his music, as if he was so determined to exhaust every possible scrap of mineral from a particular vein that he has forgotten his performers, and exhausts them too. Yet for the vastness of his range and compass, we accept this. He can write music on a scale so monumental that in that only Beethoven surpasses him, and then produce a melody of rare gentleness and intimacy, and all within the same work; the Suite No. 3 in D is an example of this, where the majestic effect of the high trumpets in the opening bars unites Baroque music and architecture, and then the well loved *Air on the G string* assures us of our humanity once more.

If one had to indicate where the essential Bach was to be found, the answer would probably be in the organ music; that was the point of departure, after all, and certainly some of the purest Bach, in strictly musical terms, is to be found there; others, perhaps, would point to keyboard works such as *The Well-tempered Clavier* or the *Goldberg Variations*, or the even purer music of *The Musical Offering* or *The*

RIGHT Thomas Hudson's portrait of Handel (1685–1759), painted in 1747.

BELOW J. S. Bach focused all his talents in the last years of his career on the task of improving the standard of Church music in Leipzig. Here we see the Thomaskirche and Thomasschule in Leipzig before rebuilding in 1732.

Art of Fugue. Even when being didactic Bach can surprise us with his achievements, which is surely a mark of genius. He had a certain musical modesty, too: having caught our attention with a perfectly good tune of his own, he then allowed it to be eclipsed by the tune of the Advent chorale, *Wachet auf*! One could hardly imagine Beethoven, let alone Wagner, doing that. The gems are distributed throughout his works, however, and to focus only on the organ music would mean ignoring the choral and vocal splendours – not to mention the orchestral items, and those from a composer who was considered to be a very competent Church musician, but little more. How much poorer the world would have been without the flute music, the cello music, or the slow movement of the double violin concerto, for example. Perhaps Schumann best summed it up when he said 'Music owes as much to Bach as a religion owes to its founder'. The letters B A C H (H corresponds to B, and B to B flat in German notation) have provided the theme for several compositions, and the name itself, which means 'brook' or 'fountain', seems particularly appropriate for a man who has been and continues to be an endless source of inspiration to composers and music-lovers alike.

Handel presents a very different face from Bach. He was, in fact, a true cosmopolitan, eighteenth-century man, and adjusted with amazing facility to the requirements of the society in which he found himself at any given time. Though German by birth, he was musically Italian in spirit, and he became English by naturalization. As distinct from Bach, he had a very wide musical education from an early age, and as well as learning the art of counterpoint and harmony, he could play the violin, oboe, organ and harpsichord. In fact he was one of the most accomplished performers on the harpsichord in the whole of Europe.

After completing a course in law at Halle University on his father's insistence, Handel became a member of the musical staff of the opera house in Hamburg, playing the violin and harpsichord. This was excellent experience, and gave him a very early insight into the workings of opera, so much so that by the time he was twenty he had written two operas of his own. It also inspired him to visit Italy, to see opera on its home ground. As an early example of his ability to adapt to circumstances, when Handel arrived in Rome opera was banned by a papal decree, so he wrote a cantata – *Apollo e Dafne* – instead. Outside Rome, however, he put on two operas, *Rodrigo* in Florence and *Agrippina* in Venice. Venice was taken by storm and *Agrippina* lasted for twenty-seven nights, an unheard-of 'run' by the standards of the time. On his return to Germany, Handel decided to go to England, where he arrived in 1710. The moment was ripe for the introduction of Italian opera, and Handel seized it. The following year he wrote *Rinaldo* in two weeks, and not only established his reputation decisively, but also produced his best opera so far. What Handel had written was not merely another example of the form known as *opera seria*, developed by Alessandro Scarlatti, but a real

The famous *castrato* singer Carlo Broschi, known as Farinelli (1705–82), shown here in caricature in 'an Oriental role'.

ABOVE Two more stars of eighteenth-century opera, 'La Beccheretta' and the castrato Nicolò Grimaldi, known as Nicolini, who was Handel's first Rinaldo.

RIGHT An etched caricature *c.* 1723 by John Vanderbank of a scene from a Handel opera of that year, probably *Flavio*, with Senesino (left), Cuzzoni (centre), and Berenstadt (right) in the title role.

psychological drama in musical terms, and the drama was expressed through the voice.

In 1717 Handel accepted the post of Master of Music to the Duke of Chandos, who had a large mansion just outside London where he lived in almost royal state. For the Duke's establishment Handel composed the *Chandos Anthems* and the pastoral *Acis and Galatea*, as well as a masque entitled *Haman and Mordecai* which, as *Esther*, became his first oratorio in 1732. His operas had almost always been artistic, if not financial, successes, but there was professional jealousy and rivalry in the operatic world, and the worry of remaining solvent into the bargain prompted Handel to judge that the time had come to give the public a change of fare. When he considered the nature of the *opera seria* he decided that the drama was essential, but that the *secco* (operatic style) recitatives could almost be dispensed with, thus throwing the arias into prominence even more. At the same time he added the chorus, because by then he was well aware of the English love of choral singing. This was not simply an additional element, however, for the chorus plays an essential part in the unfolding of the drama in his oratorios, commenting on the action and giving colour to characterization.

Handel had made the right choice between opera and oratorio, for although there was a period when he was involved in both, it was oratorio that was to carry him to his masterpiece, *Messiah*, in 1742, and occupy him almost exclusively until his death in 1759. Oddly enough *Messiah*, for all its popularity – and it is still one of the few works virtually assured of filling a hall – is not a characteristic Handel oratorio: although he used a dramatic style to interpret the words, his treatment of the theme is completely static, and in that respect not at all dramatic. All his other oratorios are more or less operas in English on a sacred theme, though even that statement needs qualification, for a work such as *Solomon* is first and foremost a profound exploration of the threefold nature of its subject, King Solomon, and, by extension, of man himself.

It has been said that if Bach's artistic home was the Church, then Handel's was the theatre, but to say that is to ignore his organ concertos, his *concerti grossi*, his keyboard music *en bloc*, and his trio sonatas, as well as his exquisite Italian cantatas with obbligato instrumental accompaniment. And yet one comes somewhat reluctantly to the conclusion that Handel, in giving so much, gave all, and that he represented the end of the Baroque tradition. One goes to him to be charmed, even delighted – and also to admire – but for renewal and inspiration in strictly musical terms one must go to Bach.

We have just considered two giants who would have demanded recognition in any age, but now it was inevitable that the path of music should be directed by individuals. Before moving on to the next stage of that progress, however, there are some important developments that must be taken into account, especially in the field of vocal and instrumental music.

Hogarth's engraving 'The Chorus', illustrating part of Willem de Fesch's lost oratorio *Judith*, of 1733. De Fesch knew Handel, and directed performances of his works.

Vocal and instrumental developments

We have seen how opera developed in Italy in the later Baroque period, and the various ways in which it was taken up in France, England and Germany. Hamburg was in fact the first city outside Venice to have a public opera house, which opened in 1678. Despite some early indications of a native product, especially in northern Germany, Italian influence tended to prevail in the end. Another form closely related to opera was the cantata, which was usually for solo voices and consisted of a series of recitatives and arias – perhaps two or three – with some form of continuo accompaniment. The cantata was never intended to be staged, but was a much more intimate affair for performance in a private house. Nevertheless within its scaled-down form there was ample scope for the performer to exhibit a wide range of vocal talent and contrasting emotions. A variant of the cantata was the serenata, which might involve two or more singers and a greater number of instrumentalists. It was admirably suited to slightly larger gatherings, perhaps in the open air, and was an appropriate but not too demanding way for a composer to honour a patron's birthday or wedding, or the birth of his children.

The church cantata, especially in the hands of Bach, became a much more extended work, and often involved soloists, chorus and orchestra, with the chorus introducing a chorale on occasion – especially when there was one that was associated with a particular season of the Church's year. Although in the Roman Catholic Church some composers went on writing in the style of Palestrina, the techniques of the opera house and of concerted music in general made increasing inroads, in a way that would have been a cause for scandal to earlier generations of clerics. Of course the cantatas and Passions of Bach were never part of the liturgy, but the time was

A clavichord in the Victoria & Albert Museum, London, made by Barthold Fritz in Brunswick in 1751. It has a treble compass of an unusual range for its time.

coming when the Mass itself would be treated in this manner. To say whether this was good or bad in musical terms is irrelevant, though to some people it is a matter of deep regret that subsequent generations made a rigid distinction between what was suitable and what was unsuitable as Church music. At its best, cantata and oratorio provided a synthesis of styles that we have never been able to recapture, and the Church has been the loser.

In the sphere of keyboard music, profound developments took place during the eighteenth century. At the start of it the principal keyboard instruments were the organ and the harpsichord, and at its end the pianoforte had arrived and was well on its way to becoming the instrument we know today. At the beginning of the century composers were writing fugues and chorale variations, and at the end of it they were writing rondos and sonatas. Such developments radically altered not only keyboard techniques but also the relationship between the keyboard instruments and other instruments.

Today we tend to take for granted the fact that the pianist has enormous scope for expression in the way he touches the keys. This sensitivity is further extended by the use of the pedals, which do not make the instrument louder or softer, but either dampen the strings or allow them to vibrate freely; the effect of a third pedal, as on some grand pianos, is to strike only one of the strings provided for any given note. A harpsichord, however, embodies no such possibilities

A square piano made in London in 1786 by Buntebart and Sievers. Whereas the shape relates back to that of the clavichord opposite, the mechanical function of the pedal to lift the dampers was to become a permanent feature of the piano.

Carl Philipp Emanuel Bach,
Kapellmeister und Musikdirektor in Hamburg.

Aus Hochachtung gezeichnet und gestochen von A. Stöttrup.

C. P. E. Bach (1714–88), son of Johann Sebastian, spent most of his working life in Berlin and Hamburg, and was an important performer and composer of keyboard music.

of gradation of tone, and indeed the only way in which one can alter the tone is by changing a stop, which causes the strings to be plucked at a different point, but even this can only be done at a suitable moment in the music. The harpsichord cannot vie with the piano dynamically, in other words in loudness or softness. An attempt was made to introduce what was known as a Venetian swell on some of the later harpsichords, in imitation of the organ swell box, but by then the piano had already displaced the harpsichord. With the organ the problems were basically much the same, except that the variety of stops was greater, and the swell box, when it was finally introduced, a considerable help. Generally, however, the effect of *crescendo* and *diminuendo* – getting loud and then soft – had to be written into the

RIGHT A French horn made by M. A. Raoux in Paris *c.* 1826. It is a particularly handsome instrument, with a green lacquer design inside the bell, and once belonged to the virtuoso Giovanni Puzzi (1792–1876).

BELOW A wind instrument known as a serpent, made in London by Gerock and Wolf *c.* 1831, and a late sixteenth-century cornett, probably Italian, made of ivory. The bottom instrument is also a cornett, made of boxwood covered with leather. Either Italian or German, it dates from the late sixteenth or early seventeenth century.

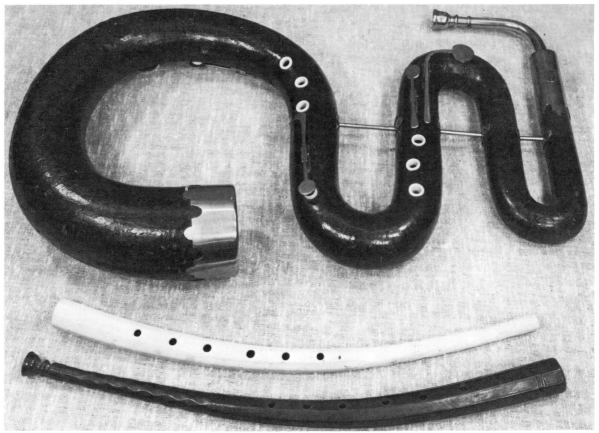

music itself. These considerations make us appreciate more readily how skilful Bach was in creating his effects essentially through the music itself. Admittedly he had a potentially expressive keyboard instrument at his disposal in the clavichord, which unlike the harpsichord is not a plucked-string instrument but a percussive one, since the strings are struck by brass tangents when the keys are depressed, and variations of tone can be obtained, though within a very restricted range. However, the clavichord could only ever be an intimate instrument, and could scarcely be used in conjunction with others. Something else was needed to carry on the keyboard tradition so brilliantly revealed by Couperin and Rameau, and taken to an extraordinary degree of virtuosity in the works of Domenico Scarlatti (1685–1757), which also prefigure, incidentally, the sonata that was to appear towards the end of the century. In fact experiments with a form of percussive harpsichord, or pianoforte as it became, had been carried out by Cristofori in Florence at the very beginning of the century, but naturally it took time to develop, let alone to be accepted and taken up by composers.

Luckily such a person existed in Carl Philipp Emanuel Bach (1714–88). Although his favourite keyboard instrument remained the clavichord, he set out, in his treatise on the playing of keyboard instruments, the rudiments of the pianoforte technique – as opposed to that of the harpsichord – and in so doing paved the way for it to supplant the harpsichord completely. As the instrument improved, makers responded to the opportunities presented by composers, and composers likewise responded to the possibilities offered by the instrument. The way was opened up for a new concept of the concerto in which the keyboard instrument would no longer be simply part of the continuo, or even first among equals, as in Bach's Fifth Brandenburg Concerto, for example; soon the piano would take its place as the solo instrument in the concerto.

The orchestra itself had been undergoing considerable change during this period, and under Lully the Paris orchestra gained a reputation for *raideur*, or strictness, that spread through Europe. Much of the strictness may have lain simply in the fact that its members played particularly well together, but no doubt their attack, too, was far from common at the time. Without this, however, the excellence of modern orchestral technique could not have been achieved, since until instrumentalists can play together and in time they cannot introduce the variations of tempo and volume that make for expressive interpretation, which was one of the main characteristics of the Classical period. Strictness, then, was not opposed to expressive orchestral playing, but on the contrary made it possible. This was seen most vividly in the orchestra at Mannheim, in Germany, where the combination of an enlightened ruler, excellent players, and composers who responded to the situation, resulted in a brilliant period of orchestral history that greatly contributed to the evolution of the symphony in its classical form. The dynamics –

The palace of Schönbrunn, Vienna, as depicted by Carl Schütz in 1782. As the eighteenth century progressed, Vienna increasingly became the focal point of music in Europe, and the importance of its role in the transition to the full development of the classical style was sealed by the two giants Haydn and Mozart.

degrees of volume of sound – and the *crescendo* and *diminuendo* achieved at Mannheim were virtually unknown at that time anywhere else in Europe.

As the eighteenth century drew on, all the elements were present for the emergence of the Classical style. The Baroque style did not, of course, suddenly come to an end in 1750. Already by about 1720 there was a move, especially in France, towards the Rococo style, or *style galant* as it is also known, and then later – largely under German influence, as we have seen – there was a movement towards the expressive style. It was not a case of these two tendencies overwhelming the other and then producing Classicism, however, for the two converged. This can be seen very well in the way in which the harpsichord gave way to the much more expressive pianoforte, after taking the *style galant* to its climax. The expressiveness offered by the new instrument was totally at one with the new spirit abroad.

The musical initiative now passed from Italy once and for all and took root in Vienna. In terms of composers and performers of opera, Italy still had much to offer until well into the next century, but in terms of progress she had now given everything she had. All this took time, of course, and the whole image of Italy as the fount of music lingered on. It was certainly strong enough for Mozart's father to think it worth his son's while to take Italy by storm, as so many northerners had done in the past, but it was to Vienna first and foremost that the musical world now turned.

4. The Classical Style

The eighteenth century was essentially a cosmopolitan age, and this was as true of the arts, and music in particular, as of anything else. Michel Paul Gui de Chabanon, writing in 1785, asserted: 'Today there is but one music in all of Europe ... this universal language of our continent.' Hand in hand with this went a great popularizing of music. The eighteenth century saw the rise of public concerts in most of the chief cities of Europe, and the failure of the old system of patronage. It survived in some places for considerably longer, but it was now possible for a composer such as Mozart to contemplate a career without the support – or constraint – of a permanent post in the service of the Church or of a royal or aristocratic patron, and although Mozart himself failed to establish financial independence, it was possible for someone like Beethoven to succeed.

The popularization of music meant that it reached, and indeed was consciously aimed at, a much wider public. A vast amount of music was published with the gifted amateur in mind, and the public's desire to know about new works and their performers led to the rise of musical journalism. Handel's friend Johann Mattheson (1681–1764) produced the first German musical periodical with his *Critica Musica* of 1722 and 1725. It can be very amusing, and sometimes astonishing, to read articles by some of the early commentators: among the composers they praised many have long since been forgotten, and in their assessments of the works of those whom we admire today, they could be notoriously wrong. But at least they served a useful purpose in bringing music to a wider public.

Trends in music, and people's expectations of it, were similar throughout Europe in the late eighteenth century. Of course national prejudices continued to exist to a certain extent, but these were only of minor relevance when we look at the overall picture. All generalizations are dangerous, but it is fair to say that the music of the mid- and late eighteenth century was expected to be both uplifting and entertaining, expressive and controlled; not too complicated or technical to be of instant appeal to the average music-lover; and

The great popularity of music-making at all levels of society in the eighteenth century stimulated the organization of clubs such as this one at Darmstadt, painted at an open-air gathering *c.* 1750 by Johann Christian Fiedler (1697–1765).

Christoph Willibald
Gluck (1714–87), as
painted by Duplessis in
1776. The portrait is now
in the Kunsthistorisches
Museum, Vienna.

above all it had to speak in a language that was truly international, or
even supranational. Of all the music of this period – and there was an
enormous amount of it – the four composers who best represent
the Classical period are Gluck, Haydn, Mozart and the young
Beethoven.

Underpinning the outward, public face of the work of these men
was a common currency of forms in which they wrote their music.
Admittedly Beethoven wrote only one complete opera (*Leonora*, later
called *Fidelio*), and the operas of Haydn, though charming when
sympathetically staged, do not strike us as great music; Gluck on the
other hand is chiefly remembered today as an operatic composer,
while Mozart is unsurpassed in the realm of opera. Together,

however, they show us the various developments of opera during the period, which by and large were convergent rather than divergent, as we shall see in the next section. When we come to instrumental music, leaving aside Gluck, the fact that all three men – Haydn, Mozart and Beethoven – wrote string quartets, sonatas, concertos and symphonies shows that it is possible to talk freely of an international language. At the heart of their music was the concept known as sonata form, which is somewhat confusing since we also have the form called sonata in its own right. The alternative name of 'first movement form' would perhaps be less confusing, but the other is so well established that it seems unlikely to be dislodged. Since it relates directly to much of the instrumental music written by composers of this period, and above all to the three mentioned above, we must look at it more closely.

Sonata form

The usual definition of sonata form is that it has a first section or exposition, which is usually repeated, and which has a first theme or perhaps group of themes in the tonic or home key in which the music is written. There follows a more lyrical theme in the dominant, the key starting on the fifth note of the tonic scale, or the relative major key, and then a closing theme which is also in the dominant or the relative major. There may be a transitional or bridge passage between the different themes. The second section or development section takes themes from the exposition or first section and treats them in a different way, and may move into different keys. The third section is known as the recapitulation, in the course of which the material of the first section is heard again in its original order, but all the themes are now in the tonic or home key once more. There may also be a final section known as the coda.

This definition did not really emerge until the decade after Beethoven's death, and was therefore intended, for those proposing to practise it, as a summary of what sonata form had come to mean by then. It was not seen as a summing-up of all that had gone before. For one thing, most of Haydn's sonatas hardly fit into this scheme; for another, the individual genius of a given composer was bound to make itself felt in many different ways. In general, though, sonata form was used by Haydn, Mozart and Beethoven for so much of their instrumental music that a basic understanding of it is of fundamental importance. In particular, sonata form has to be taken into account for the development of the symphony in its fullest expression in the Classical form.

We have already seen how the rise of the orchestral tradition at Mannheim paved the way for important developments in orchestral technique, and we shall look at instrumental developments generally in the next section. Here we are concerned chiefly with the form, and Mannheim, with its orchestra of what Burney described as 'an army of generals', was an important centre in Germany – though there were others at Berlin and, of course, Vienna. It was in Vienna that the great trio of Haydn, Mozart and Beethoven made much of their contribution to the musical tradition. We shall now examine the lives and careers of Haydn and Mozart, and leave Beethoven to a later section.

Haydn

Franz Joseph Haydn (1732–1809) was born into a poor family in eastern Austria, near the border with Hungary. At the age of six he went to live with an uncle who taught him the rudiments of music, and two years later he became a chorister at St Stephen's Cathedral in Vienna. Although he gained much practical musical experience at this time, he was given no lessons in the more theoretical side, so that when his voice broke there was no logical course open for him to pursue. He managed to earn his living, however, by doing some teaching and a variety of odd jobs, while teaching himself counterpoint from Fux's *Gradus ad Parnassum*. He did in fact have some lessons from Nicola Porpora (1686–1768), the singing teacher and composer, and began to make a name for himself in Vienna, where there were plenty of rich aristocrats who were prepared to patronize music and musicians. He obtained a post as *Kapellmeister* to the Bohemian nobleman Count von Morzin in 1758, and it was for the Count's orchestra that Haydn wrote his first symphony. However, this appointment gave way to a much more important one

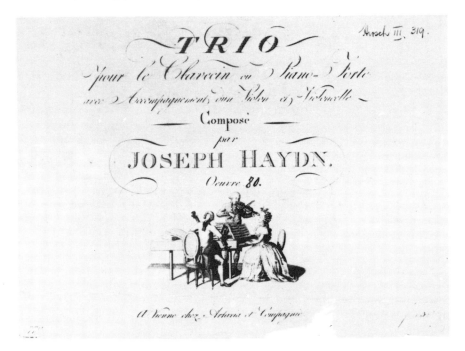

The title page of Haydn's trio, Opus 80, for violin, cello and keyboard, published by Artaria in Vienna. Note that the keyboard instrument is specified as being either harpsichord or pianoforte – a sign of the changing times.

HANOVER-SQUARE.

MR. HAYDN respectfully acquaints the No-
bility and Gentry, that his CONCERT will be on
This Day, the 16th of May.

Part I. New Grand Overture, Haydn. Aria, Signora
Storace. New Concertante for Violin, Oboe, Flute, and Obli-
gata, Messrs. Salomon, Harrington, and Caravoglio – Haydn.
New Aria (with Oboe and Bassoon Obligata) Signor David—
Haydn. Concerto Violin, Signor Giornovichi.

Part II. (By particular desire) the new Grand Overture,
Haydn, as performed at Mr. Salomon's first Concert. Sonata,
Signor Pacchierotti—Haydn. Concertante for Piano Forte
and Pedal Harp, Mr. Dusseck and Madame Krumpholtz.
Duetto, Signor David and Signor Pacchierotti. Finale, Haydn.

Doors to be opened at Seven, and begin exactly at Eight
o'Clock.

Tickets, at Half-a-Guinea each, to be had of Mr. Haydn,
No. 18, Great Pulteney-street, Golden-square; at Messrs.
Longman and Broderip's, Cheapside and Haymarket; and at
Mr. Bland's Music Warehouse, No. 45, Holborn.

An advertisement, dated Monday 16 May 1791, for one of the Haydn-Salomon concerts given in London during Haydn's first visit to the city.

in 1761, when Haydn entered the service of the Hungarian Prince Paul Anton Esterházy. It was in the service of this man, and of his brother Nicholas who succeeded him in 1762, that Haydn spent almost the next thirty years of his life, with a small orchestra and an opera company permanently at his disposal.

From 1766 Prince Esterházy spent most of his time on his country estate, but his palace was sumptuous, with two music rooms and a theatre for opera, so there was plenty of scope for Haydn. His patron would join in the music-making, playing the baryton, an instrument like a large viola da gamba with sympathetic vibrating strings. This accounts for the fact that Haydn wrote almost two hundred pieces for the instrument. It might seem, then, that Haydn, removed to a remote part of Hungary, and forced to write pieces for a somewhat archaic instrument to please his patron, could have been in danger of isolation from the main stream of musical life, and indeed the operas that he wrote for Esterházy are by no means modern, even by the standards of their own time. However, he went to Vienna from time to time, and the Prince frequently received visitors at the palace. As Haydn himself wrote, with no little perception:

My prince was pleased with all my work, I was commended, and as conductor of an orchestra I could make experiments, observe what strengthened and what weakened an effect and improve thereupon, substitute, omit, and try new things. I was cut off from the world, there was no one around to mislead and harass me, and so I was forced to become original.

It is hardly surprising, then, that Haydn was content to stay in the Prince's service, despite the fact that the terms of his contract prevented him from even giving away any of his compositions, let alone from selling them. In spite of his apparent isolation, his fame began to spread, and as it did so, the terms of the contract were overlooked, and Haydn was able to accept commissions from the rest of Europe.

When the Prince died in 1790, Haydn settled in Vienna for a while, but in collaboration with the impresario Salomon he spent two seasons in London – during the course of which the twelve London symphonies were composed – from January 1791 to July 1792, and from February 1794 to August 1795. After that he returned to the Esterházy family in the service of the new Prince, Nicholas II, who was less of a musician than his father, but was pleased to have the

A gouache dating from 1775 by an unknown artist showing a performance of Haydn's opera *L'incontro improvviso* at Esterháza. It is possibly the composer at the keyboard in the pit.

Haydn's oratorio *The Creation*, which was given in the great hall of Vienna University in 1808. The scene was painted by Balthasar Wigand on a wooden casket that was presented to Haydn by Princess Herminegild Esterházy but unfortunately destroyed in the Second World War.

renowned Haydn in his service. The chief products of this period as far as Haydn's music was concerned were the six Masses written from 1796 to 1802, and the two oratorios, *The Creation* and *The Seasons*, which were performed in Vienna in 1798 and 1801 respectively with great success. There were also his remarkable string quartets, his last composition being the String Quartet Opus 103, of which he completed only two movements.

It was in the two forms of the string quartet and the symphony that Haydn made his chief contribution to the future of music. He also wrote a considerable body of Church music, but the best of it is infused with symphonic elements, so that it ranks with the symphony. His career was entirely unspectacular, and in complete antithesis to what one might have expected of a person who was readily acknowledged as probably the greatest composer of his day. He knew how to write attractively for the public, however, without ever compromising his artistic integrity, and he worked out his solutions and achieved his progress only through very conscientious work. In so doing he left behind him not only a large amount of delightful and rewarding music, but handed on to his successors for years to come a solid foundation on which they in turn might build their music.

Mozart

Haydn's immediate successor was Wolfgang Amadeus Mozart (1756–91), who was born in Salzburg, at the opposite end of Austria to Haydn, a city that in those days was ruled by an archbishop within the Holy Roman Empire. By contrast with the atmosphere in which Haydn grew up, Salzburg in Mozart's day was blessed with a long and distinguished musical tradition, and his father Leopold was a member of the archbishop's chapel, as well as the author of a famous treatise on violin-playing. Mozart revealed a talent for music at a very early age, and it was as a musical prodigy, along with his sister Nannerl, that his father took him on a series of tours that included France, England, Holland and Italy, as well as some of the most important cities of Germany, and Vienna itself. He soon became a virtuoso keyboard performer and a fine violinist, and his composing career was no less impressive. By the time he was six he was composing minuets, and had written his first symphony before he was nine. His first oratorio was written when he was eleven, and his first opera at the ripe age of twelve.

Mozart was therefore exposed to the demands of composition very early on, and through his travels was aware of most of the music that was being written and played throughout western Europe at that crucial stage of his formative years. In this respect he was totally unlike Haydn, who forged his own style with few external influences. Mozart represents a kind of synthesis of almost everything that he

encountered, which gave his music its truly cosmopolitan flavour. Over and above that, of course, there was his own genius. Very often the output of a composer may be seen in direct relationship to the events of his personal life, or of the world around him. This was especially true of the Romantic composers, and indeed it became almost a hallmark of the Romantic experience. But although Mozart had a difficult private life, and lived in a time of considerable upheaval caused by the imminent French Revolution and new philosophical concepts, none of this may be detected directly in his music; even where ideas are articulated, as in the libretti of some of the operas, the music really transcends the texts, and Mozart's psychological penetration makes the portrayal of the characters themselves of more interest than the more transitory demands that are made by the plot.

Again in contrast to Haydn, Mozart found composition very easy, thanks largely to his sound training, and his ability to elaborate his ideas in his mind before committing them to paper. Of course he was obliged to work hard at some of his compositions, especially – ironically enough – the six string quartets that he published in 1785 and dedicated to Haydn in gratitude for all that he had learnt from him. Broadly speaking, his career may be divided into three periods: his childhood and youth up to 1774; his first masterworks between 1774 and 1781; and lastly the period in Vienna from 1781 until his death ten years later.

Mozart's earliest opera, written when he was twelve, was in fact an *opera buffa, La finta semplice*, to a libretto of Goldoni. In the same year he composed *Bastien und Bastienne* which, as its name implies, was something of a hybrid. Although it was in German, and therefore qualifies for the German term *singspiel*, the original inspiration for the libretto had been Rousseau's *Le devin du village*, so that it could also be regarded as an *opéra comique*. He then moved on to two heroic themes in the *opera seria* tradition, namely *Mitridate* (1770) and *Lucio Silla* (1772), but he was not ready for such a large leap, and returned to *opera buffa* with *La finta giardiniera* (1774–5). *Il rè pastore* (1775), though described as a '*dramma per musica*', still did not give him the scope that he was looking for. As he complained somewhat bitterly, '. . . some people think one remains twelve all one's life'.

Relief was at hand, however, for at the age of twenty-five he was commissioned to write a big *opera seria* for Munich. The result was *Idomeneo*, composed during the winter of 1780–1 and first performed on 29 January 1781. For Mozart it was the most significant event in his career so far; he himself regarded it as one of his masterpieces, and he tried persistently but in vain to get it mounted again. Although in *Idomeneo* Mozart was patently influenced by Gluck, at the same time he broke new ground, for instance in his use of the chorus. Unfortunately, however, the *opera seria* had had its day, and although he returned to it at the very end of his life with *La clemenza di Tito* (1791), the intervening period had shown that Mozart's operatic talents were to be deployed elsewhere.

ABOVE Wolfgang Amadeus Mozart (1756–91) in an unfinished portrait (1782–3) by Joseph Lange, now in the Mozart Museum, Salzburg.

LEFT The playbill for the first Viennese performance of *Don Giovanni*, given by command of Emperor Joseph II.

LEFT The entrance of the Queen of the Night in the Mozart opera *Die zauberflöte*, in the set for the 1818 production in Munich designed by Simon Quaglio.

BELOW The old Burgtheater in the Michaelerplatz in Vienna. Under Joseph II it became the National Theatre, and several Mozart operas were first staged here, notably *Die entführung*, *Le nozze di Figaro* and *Così fan tutte*.

The moment in *Don Giovanni* when the protagonist is finally carried off to Hell: a representation of the first performance in Prague.

In fact the next opera, *Die entführung aus dem serail* (1781–2) was a complete change of direction. It was written in response to the encouragement given by Emperor Joseph II to the establishment of a national tradition of opera in Vienna to counteract Italian and French influences. Mozart did not settle very easily to the task demanded of him, and *Die entführung* was not a great success, but it paved the way for two of his greatest operas, *Le nozze di Figaro* (1785–6) and *Don Giovanni* (1787). On one level *Figaro* is in the direct line of *opera buffa*, but the interplay of personalities, translated into musical and dramatic terms, sets it far above any of its predecessors. *Don Giovanni* takes this development even further, and it is enriched by Mozart's own experience and views of human nature. It was his fascination with, and readiness to record in musical terms, all the facets of human nature that marked out Mozart, in contrast to Beethoven, as an operatic composer. Of course Beethoven said very profound things about humanity, but they tended to be somewhat abstract by comparison with the statements of Mozart.

After *Don Giovanni* some people have found *Così fan tutte* (1790) rather artificial, and even cynical, despite the fact that it includes some of Mozart's most beautiful music. Such criticism stems usually from those who like to see a continuing development in a composer's work, and who therefore are unable to conceive that Mozart simply responded to Da Ponte's libretto – which is arguably his best – and produced something that was sheer delight. Of course, Mozart did not simply abandon his critical faculties while he was writing *Così fan tutte*, and for all its apparent lightness, it expressed profound human emotion in very telling terms; those who require a deep interpretation for the opera as a whole usually tend to see it, therefore, as an allegory.

There is certainly some justification for this view in the light of Mozart's last opera, *Die zauberflöte* (1791), which is a *singspiel* – although in name only, for it is a synthesis of elements from almost all the vocal and operatic traditions that had gone before, transmitted by Mozart into what is the first and also one of the greatest of German operas. It is an allegory, not only directly in terms of Schikaneder's libretto, which is concerned with Masonic enlightenment and Roman Catholic obscurantism, but on a much deeper plane, for it explores the struggle between the darkness and light inside each one of us. The framework of the *singspiel*, however, ensures that this theme is not dealt with on an abstract, grandiose level, but on a very human one – Mozart himself declared, 'I deem nothing human alien to me'. How very different from the operatic world of Haydn, whose serene horizons are never darkened by such intense considerations. But then the careers of the two men are full of contrasts, in life and in death; nothing could be more different than the manner of their ends, for whereas Haydn went, at a ripe old age, to an honoured grave, Mozart was consigned as a pauper to an unmarked one.

Opera apart, when we look at the output of the two men, there is

little to choose between them as far as the symphony and the quartet are concerned, but it is to the concerto – and especially the piano concerto – that Mozart made his greatest contribution. The Venetian composer Vivaldi, who died in Vienna in 1741, established the form of the concerto in three movements, consisting of fast outer sections enclosing a slow central section, the first movement usually longer and musically more weighty than the other two. The older concerto tended to proceed with a regular alternation of the solo instrument with the other instrumental forces involved, but what Mozart did was to treat both elements more or less equally, so that they were seen as complementing each other in the overall texture, rather than as two individual elements contributing to the total effect. This gave a much richer field of possibilities for texture and contrast, and one that Mozart delighted to explore. Of course he was an accomplished pianist himself, whereas Vivaldi's solo instrument had been the violin, much closer in sound to the orchestral body, and therefore less easy to blend and still retain its soloistic character.

There were formal problems, too, so that Vivaldi's concertos tend

ABOVE The opening of Mozart's 'Dissonance' quartet in C, K.465. The name was not given by Mozart, of course, but by subsequent musicians intrigued by the curiously dissonant chords at the beginning of the work.

ABOVE LEFT Mozart's handwritten copy of the motet 'God is our refuge', which he gave to the relatively young British Museum in July 1765.

LEFT Title page of an 1802 edition of Mozart's 'Musical Joke', K.522, composed in Vienna on 14 June 1787.

to be much shorter, and the ways of elaborating thematic material available to Mozart were unknown to Vivaldi, who would surely have delighted in the possibilities of orchestral texture open to Mozart and developed by him. There are some parallels in their careers, however, that are interesting to note. Both Mozart and Vivaldi had troubled relations with their employers, but while Vivaldi was able to make a financial success of most of his life, Mozart had to struggle in order to establish himself as an independent composer in his own right. For this reason, coupled with his ability, if that is the term, to write such sublime music, he became something of a hero for the Romantic composers who followed. He made it possible for the composer to follow his artistic dictates, and although Beethoven complained bitterly at times about what he regarded as his servitude, he vindicated what Mozart had attempted to do but had failed so tragically to achieve. Before coming to the last of the three giants – Beethoven himself – we shall look at the realms of opera and Church music, and the developments that had taken place in instrumental technique and writing.

Eighteenth-century opera

During the earlier part of the eighteenth century the operatic style that had emanated from Venice in the Baroque period still held sway in much of Germany, and in England too, whereas in France there was little change from what had already been established. When progress came it was of the same sort that had directed instrumental music – a move towards music that appealed to the audience, that was as simple and natural as possible, and that had the widest possible appeal. It was, therefore, cosmopolitan too.

The plots of early operas usually revolved around two pairs of lovers, and the story of their final union in marital bliss allowed for a variety of situations and adventures that might include pastoral or nautical scenes, military encounters, and civic and religious ceremonies. Usually the plot would be resolved by a heroic deed or the renunciation of one lover by another, or sometimes the intervention of a ruler or supernatural agency. All this took place in three acts, the story being carried forward in the recitatives, and the

Pietro Domenico Olivero's impression of a scene in Francesco Feo's opera *Arsace*, which was given at the Teatro Reggio in Turin in 1740–1.

An engraving by Birckart of Giuseppe Galli-Bibiena's design for Fux's *Costanza e Fortezza*, which was given in Prague Castle in 1723 in celebration of the coronation of Charles VI as King of Bohemia. The title of the opera – which means Constancy and Fortitude – was the Emperor's motto. More than three hundred singers and instrumentalists took part, and the performance lasted from eight in the evening until one in the morning.

dramatic situation being summed up in the arias that followed them. Occasionally there were duets, but very rarely any ensembles or choruses of importance. The role of the orchestra was chiefly restricted to the overture and to accompanying the arias, since the recitatives were generally only accompanied by harpsichord and bass. Occasionally some recitatives had orchestral accompaniment for special effects. It can be seen from this brief resumé that it was the arias that bore much of the musical burden, and in particular the *da capo* aria. The words '*da capo*' mean 'from the beginning again', and this was indeed the way the aria was constructed: after the first section a slower one followed, which might well be in a different key; the third section would repeat the first, but with added embellishment by the singer.

The form of the *opera seria*, as this was called, was thus established early. It was highly conventional, and in the face of a general trend towards nature and a return to realism, it appeared increasingly artificial and contrived as the century progressed. It was in any case open to abuse. Benedetto Marcello wrote an anonymous satire on *opera seria* as early as 1720, but it was only much later that any changes were actually made. For one thing, there was so much musical emphasis on the arias that they became merely vehicles for the singers to show off their talents, and since operas depended very much on the 'star system' as we would call it today, this only encouraged the singers to even greater extravagances. They held the librettists, composers and impresarios to ransom by demanding arias that would show off their particular talents irrespective of the sentiments appropriate to the plot, and costumes and props that were designed solely to enhance their appearance, with scant reference to the characters they were meant to be portraying. Such requirements were even written into the contracts, and music became, sadly, almost the last consideration in the whole business.

Perhaps one of the most extraordinary and yet at the same time perfectly characteristic features of *opera seria* was the role of the castrato. A castrato was a male singer who usually had a very fine voice as a boy, and was then castrated at puberty in order to try and preserve its quality. Most frequently they were sopranos, but mezzo-soprano and alto castrati were quite common. Effectively they retained the voice of a boy with the lungs of an adult, and from accounts of their performances it would certainly seem that they had phenomenal breath control, and that their voices were unusually penetrating. The musical historian Charles Burney recorded an incident when Farinelli was appearing in an opera in Naples, and one of his arias was accompanied by a trumpet. The show literally stopped each night, the aria degenerating into a competition between singer and instrumentalist, egged on by the audience, to see which had the greater breath control, and could introduce the most florid ornaments into the music. Eventually Farinelli won, though the whole affair can hardly be called an artistic experience.

Of course castrati would never have achieved the prominence they did unless the public had encouraged them, and it is significant that they never had any following in France, where they were regarded with something approaching horror. Nevertheless as fine a musical sensibility as Mozart's found the castrato voice perfectly acceptable. Vincenzo dal Prato created the role of Idamante in *Idomeneo*, and Mozart wrote the solo motet *Exsultate, jubilate* for Venanzio Rauzzini; both men were castrati. By modern standards the timbre of these voices can hardly have been beautiful, however, and it was above all the skill of the singers that commended itself to the listener, whereas a later age would prefer a more natural and doubtless more aesthetically pleasing sound. With the revival of the counter tenor voice, or male alto in a solo capacity, the idea of males singing in a high and therefore traditionally feminine register is once more acceptable. Indeed, in British cathedrals the tradition went on in unbroken succession from pre-Reformation days. These were, and are, however, completely natural voices.

The Venetian painter and architect Romoaldo Mauri designed this magnificent set for the Ascensiontide celebrations in 1753 for the stage of the Grimani Theatre of San Samuele. The glittering effect of crystal and silver impressed contemporary Venetians so much – and they certainly were not starved of such splendour – that the scene was engraved for posterity.

La magnifica Scena di Cristalli, trasparenti, movimenti e Pittura toccata d'
argento, che si ammirò nel Teatro Grimani di S. Samuele in Venezia nella Fiera
dell'Ascensione L'anno 1753. Idea del Sig.r Antonio Codognato, disegnata,
et eseguita dal Sig.r Romualdo Mauri Pittore, e Architetto Veneziano.

What is perhaps more difficult for the modern opera-goer to accept is the fact that it was perfectly usual in certain operas for female roles to be sung by castrati suitably disguised, while in others there were both castrati performing women's roles, and women performing men's roles. Of course in cities like Rome, where women were theoretically forbidden to appear on the stage, it is understandable that castrati were frequently employed, but they were also used in many places where no such restrictions were in force. In Handel's *Julius Caesar* no less than six of the nine principals are sopranos or contraltos, thus showing a definite preference for the effect of a majority of upper voices – an aesthetic, quite simply, that has vanished with the passage of time.

It was inevitable that change should come, and when it did it was towards the more cosmopolitan style. It can be appreciated in the work of two Italians, Niccolò Jommelli (1714–74) in Stuttgart and Tommaso Traetta (1727–79) in Parma, but the man who really formulated the international style was Christoph Willibald Gluck (1714–87). He was born in Bohemia, but studied with Sammartini in Italy, and after visiting England and Germany he settled in Vienna as court composer to the emperor. Since the French Queen, Marie-Antoinette, was an Austrian princess, Gluck's fame also went to Paris. His reform did not begin at once, and his early operas were in the traditional *opera seria* style, but gradually he became more and

Arne's opera *Artaxerxes* (which was a favourite of Haydn) was rudely interrupted in 1763 during a performance at Covent Garden, because the management had decided to abolish the practice of charging only half price after the third act. Irate members of the audience climbed over the pit on to the stage, to the dismay of orchestra and singers alike.

A painting by Giovanni Paolo Panini (*c.* 1692–1765) depicting a concert given in Rome in the private theatre of Cardinal de Polignac in honour of the birth of the Dauphin. The painting is in the Louvre Museum, Paris.

more sympathetic to the ideas of reform, of which the fruits were the operas *Orfeo ed Euridice* (1762) and *Alceste* (1767). These two operas show his concern to integrate the component parts of the old style into a coherent whole. Thus the division between recitative and aria was reduced, less indulgence was given to the vanity of the singers, and the orchestra was used essentially to further the dramatic development. As Gluck explained in his preface to *Alceste*, he wanted the music to serve the poetry and the plot.

When *Iphigénie en Aulide* was produced in Paris in 1774, Gluck had reached the climax of his career. It was through no fault of his that the *guerre des bouffons* had broken out in Paris in 1752, but in a new outbreak in 1774 he was able to capitalize on the fact that by then Lully and Rameau had been discredited, and there was nothing to take their place. The *bouffons* in the first battle were an Italian opera company playing in Paris, who became a focal point for the criticism of those who felt that French opera needed to take a new direction. The philosopher Jean-Jacques Rousseau (1712–78) was one of the leading spokesmen, and although his talents as a composer were limited, he wrote a piece, *Le devin du village* (1752), in support of his views. Of course Gluck's work was much more sophisticated, and by adapting Racine's tragedy in *Iphigénie* he not only complimented the French and one of their greatest playwrights, but also broke new ground in setting a French text to music. This virtually ensured his

LEFT Antoine Watteau (1684–1721) may well have set his *Music Party* against the view of the old Champs Elysées from the Tuileries, in Paris. The central figure is playing a theorbo or large lute, with two sets of strings and tuning pegs.

BELOW A painting by Nicolas Lancret (1690–1743) of Mademoiselle Camargo dancing. She and her rival, Mademoiselle Sallé, introduced many important innovations into ballet.

RIGHT Haydn
(1732–1809), as painted
by J. Ziterer.

BELOW A reconstruction,
by Adolph von Menzel
(1815–1905), of a flute
concert at Potsdam under
Frederick II, who was
taught the flute by
Joachim Quantz.

success. He quickly followed it with French versions of *Orfeo* and *Alceste*, and in 1779 produced his masterpiece, *Iphigénie en Tauride*. When the new operatic war broke out it was between the supporters of the Neapolitan composer Niccolò Piccini (1728–1800), then popular in Paris, and those of Gluck. Gluck prevailed, and in fact influenced Piccini, as well as a succession of composers such as Cherubini, Spontini, and even Berlioz in *Les Troyens*.

This was opera in its highest, most idealized Classical form, but alongside it was a much lighter opera, which tended to be a more popular and therefore more truly national genre. It began in France and Italy with the *intermezzi*, pieces inserted between the acts of a play or as curtain-raisers. Gradually the *intermezzo* became a complete entertainment in its own right, with spoken dialogue – a fully-fledged *opéra comique*. A very early form of it in England was John Gay's *Beggar's Opera* of 1728, though strictly speaking this was a ballad opera, and not quite the same as the French and Italian *opéra comique*. Even so, insofar as it represented a reaction against the dominance of foreign opera – mainly against the work of Handel in London – it may be considered part of this general trend. Perhaps it had more in common with the German version of the *intermezzo*, the *singspiel*, a tradition on which Mozart drew for some of his work. Another important German development was the *Lied*, which means simply 'song', but which eventually embraced the great stream of recital songs that Schubert, Schumann and many others developed to such a refined degree in the nineteenth century.

Church music in the eighteenth century

As secular vocal music made enormous progress, Church music was left in something of a dilemma, since those who followed the tradition of Palestrina became increasingly isolated from the main development of music. Inevitably the influence of opera began to appear in both liturgical Church music and oratorio. Soon the oratorio was barely distinguishable from opera. Indeed Handel, for instance, made a conscious attempt to fuse the two as far as possible. There was a more pronounced difference between the operas and the oratorios of Haydn, but even so it is one of character rather than of fundamental musical change. Symphonic influences were also making themselves felt in the specifically Church music of both Haydn and Mozart, and the result is more a fusion of the old and new, rather than the forging of any 'modern' style. This is perhaps what we should expect, since all the tendencies had been towards a cosmopolitan, international style; indeed many commentators, with the benefit of hindsight, feel that it is a matter of great regret that the next century brought such a sharp distinction between secular and religious music. Once that distinction had been made there was no going back, and with the increasing secularization of society it became more and more difficult for a composer who wished to dedicate his talents to God to find a suitable idiom in which to do so without either being deliberately archaic or compromising himself. It is a problem that still exists.

Orchestral innovations

At intervals the authorities tried to take practical steps to regulate the situation, and one of the reasons that Haydn wrote no Masses between about 1782 and 1796 was the existence of an imperial decree that restricted the use of orchestras for accompanying Church music. Certainly the growth of the orchestra, and the inclusion of trumpets and drums – instruments that had previously had solely military associations – alarmed those who saw the religious domain increasingly invaded by the secular one. Throughout the eighteenth century, however, the average orchestra was much smaller than it is today. In 1756 the orchestra at Mannheim had twenty violins, four violas, cellos and double basses, two flutes, oboes and bassoons, four horns, one trumpet and two kettledrums. This was far in advance of most other orchestras, and not to be taken as the norm. The average orchestra that Haydn was accustomed to between about 1760 and 1785 had slightly more than half that number of players. Even in the 1790s there were rarely more than about thirty-five members in Viennese orchestras.

Alongside this evolution of the orchestra went a development in the way composers used the forces at their disposal. It was basically a change of mentality from the *basso continuo* and harpsichord holding

RIGHT The interior of the old Opéra, Paris.

OVERLEAF:
LEFT Mozart with his sister Nannerl and father Leopold, painted by Louis Carmontelle in 1763–4. Note the old form of pike-nosed bow used by Leopold Mozart. Later bows could be much more taut, giving a clearer focus of tone and allowing firmer attack. Copies of this picture were distributed by Leopold for advertizing purposes.

RIGHT Beethoven (1770–1827) as depicted by Joseph Stieler in 1819–20, with his manuscript of the *Missa solemnis*.

LEFT A scene in a private house in Venice in the eighteenth century. The painting, by an anonymous artist, hangs in the Casa Goldoni, Venice. To most visitors it seemed as if the Venetians did nothing except make music, and indeed the longer the Republic survived, the more it seemed dedicated to such pleasures.

RIGHT Private music-making in France, captured by Jean-Honoré Fragonard (1732–1806). The trio consists of flute, horn and harp.

the ensemble at the start of the century, to much more of the work being entrusted to the strings in the middle of the century, and then the gradual disappearance of the *basso continuo* by the end. This meant that the harpsichord eventually fell out of use, and instead of the ensemble being directed from the keyboard, the task now fell to the first violin. Haydn, however, was still known on occasion to direct from the pianoforte, so deeply rooted was the tradition in his case.

Another important factor was the use of woodwind, which at first were only employed to double the string parts or fill in the harmonies, and were sometimes added even when the composer had not written anything for them to play. But as the century wore on they were taken increasingly on their own merits, and given a more important role. In a solo context, of course, they were taken up fairly quickly by composers in a way that explored their individual natures rather than as alternatives to the violin. Purcell wrote oboe solos when the instrument was a newcomer to the orchestra, and Mozart, almost a century later, was a great devotee of the clarinet when it was still relatively new. It was one thing to envisage the instruments in a solo capacity, however, and another thing entirely to incorporate them into the orchestra in their own right, not simply as contributors of more sound or volume, but for their particular colours and contribution to the overall texture. They were no longer merely an 'optional extra'.

FAR LEFT An oil sketch by Moritz von Schwind (1804–71) of a Schubert evening at Joseph von Spaun's, with the composer at the piano. In his youth Schwind had been a friend of Schubert, but made this sketch towards the end of his life, in 1868.

LEFT Brahms (1833–97) portrayed against a background of his own music, of which he was a relentless critic.

BELOW A painting by Mauzaisse, after Giroust, now at Versailles, of Madame de Genlis giving a harp lesson to her daughter and Princess Adélaïde of Orléans.

A setting by William Boyce (1710–79) of the words of 'Rural Beauty – or Vauxhal Garden', thus celebrating the famous London pleasure gardens, a picture of which appears at the top.

An interesting intermediate development between the symphony orchestra and the intimacy of the string quartet was the serenade, for example Mozart's *Eine Kleine Nachtmusik*. It might be written for strings alone or wind alone, or possibly a combination of the two. It was essentially intended for the open air or informal occasions, when it was not convenient to include a harpsichord. The music therefore had to be written differently from the traditional method with *basso continuo*, and this helped greatly in the development of the string quartet and the various forms of chamber music that evolved with it.

The basic string quartet consisted of two violins, viola and cello, which were virtually equal partners in an ensemble of such delicate balance that ever since its inception it has drawn from composers some of their finest music. It had, of course, certain precedents, for instance Purcell's fantasias, but these were isolated early examples, and not truly forerunners of the string quartet. Indeed, one might say that its development was a necessary concomitant of the trends in Classical music, so that as the symphony and the opera, the Mass and the oratorio, grew more important, so did the need for a distillation of pure music; as the sounds of the orchestra became more rich and more complex, there was a corresponding need to find a medium that

Harpsichord and cello feature in this painting of the Morse family of Aberdeen by Johann Zoffany (1733–1810), but by this time the harpsichord was rapidly losing ground to the piano.

LEFT Giuseppe Verdi (1813–1901) as a young man, in a portrait by an unknown artist. The start of Verdi's operatic career coincided with one of the most difficult periods of his life: his infant daughter died in 1838, his son in 1839, and his wife in 1840; his first opera, *Oberto*, saw the light of day in November 1839,

and the second, *Un giorno di regno*, which was an *opera buffa*, appeared in September 1840, to a disastrous reception. He did not write another comic opera until *Falstaff* – which was also his last.

ABOVE The first four and the last four operas of Verdi's long career all had their premières in the Milan opera house, La Scala, seen as it was in his time in Angelo Inganni's painting of 1852.

relied entirely on balancing individuality with equality – a truly enlightened concept in the Age of Enlightenment. There was also a practical side, of course, since the string quartet was a much more practical ensemble than an orchestra from the point of view of expense, availability of players, ease of arranging rehearsal time, and so on. Nevertheless, the significance of the string quartet for both Haydn and Mozart – and, as we shall soon see, perhaps particularly for Beethoven – indicates its fundamental importance as a musical form.

Beethoven

Ludwig van Beethoven (1770–1827) was born in Bonn, now the capital of West Germany but in those days the seat of the Elector of Cologne, ruler of the Rhine Palatinate, which was another of the quasi-autonomous regions that went to make up the Holy Roman Empire. Beethoven's grandfather had gone to Bonn from the Low Countries and became *Kapellmeister* to the Elector, and Beethoven's father was also on the musical staff there, though he was not nearly as good a musician as his father. So the boy grew up in a musical atmosphere, and though he was by no means a child prodigy like Mozart, his father recognized that he had talent, and determined to exploit it.

In those days Bonn was a civilized and, by all accounts, pleasant place to live in, but it did not offer Beethoven the experience and stimulation he needed to develop his musical talent. In 1787 he went to Vienna to seek out Mozart and perhaps to have some lessons. Unfortunately this first trip was a failure, largely because Beethoven was acutely short of money and his mother fell ill. He decided to return to Bonn, where she died shortly afterwards. It was a failure from an artistic point of view, too. Beethoven never found composition easy, whereas Mozart did and possibly could have helped Beethoven in this respect. However, in his native city Beethoven gained some useful experience playing in the Elector's orchestra for opera and ballet, and also playing the organ; and help was at hand: Haydn passed through Bonn towards the end of 1790 on his way to London for the first time, and it was he who encouraged Beethoven to think again about going to Vienna. It was difficult because he was by now virtually the family breadwinner, but for his own career he needed wider horizons than those offered by Bonn. So Beethoven returned to Vienna in 1792, and was destined never to see Bonn again.

His aim was to have lessons with Haydn in Vienna, but though Haydn was a good friend to the young Beethoven, their association was not a great success. Haydn was in any case planning a return visit to London for 1794, but, that apart, he does not seem to have been able to impart a great deal to Beethoven, who had more practical help

LEFT AND ABOVE
Sketches by Lyser of
Beethoven who, it is said,
after the attempted
suicide of his nephew
Karl, walked, and looked,
like a man of seventy.

RIGHT The Theater an
der Wien, Vienna, during
the first performance of
Fidelio in 1805. As the
French had just entered
the city, it was hardly
likely that the opera
would be heard to
advantage, and indeed it
was a flop. Beethoven
revised it for
performances in 1806,
when it had a better
reception, but still it
failed to win the
recognition that the
composer felt it deserved.

from Schenk (1753–1836), Albrechtsberger (1736–1809) and Salieri (1750–1825). Nevertheless Beethoven always held Haydn in high regard and acknowledged his greatness; though of course, in the context of musical history, Beethoven was certainly the greater genius. He lived at a propitious moment. Mozart and Haydn had handed on to him a musical style and a number of musical forms which they had considerably developed, but which still had unexplored potential. In the wider historical context, Beethoven lived in an age of enormous change, even though at first glance it seems as if the changes affected him minimally. The Bastille had been stormed in 1789; in 1792 – the year Beethoven went to Vienna for the second time – George Washington was President of the United States of America, and Goethe was in charge of the theatre at Weimar. A soldier in the French army called Napoleon Bonaparte was on his way to fame.

In the wake of the French Revolution, Beethoven's homeland disappeared for ever as an independent state, and Napoleon's arrival in Vienna caused the composer considerable inconvenience. Indeed, the failure of his opera *Leonora* at its first production was largely due to the French presence in Vienna. However, Beethoven propounded no political or philosophical views, except insofar as they affected his career and his role as an artist in society. Nevertheless, like Napoleon and Goethe, he was inescapably a child of his time, and the forces at work in Europe inevitably affected him, and made themselves felt in his work. As a composer Beethoven was steeped in the Classical tradition and was a direct product of that tradition, but because the old forms of society were crumbling and the entire role of music and the composer in relation to society was changing, both through the historical process and of course his own genius, Beethoven

metamorphosed the Classical period into the Romantic. He may be regarded, then, as the last of the Classical composers and the first of the Romantics, but he was essentially an individualist – probably the greatest composer that the West has ever seen, or ever will see.

His output was immensely varied and of an exceptional quality and scale. It includes magnificent symphonies, overtures, incidental music for the stage, violin and piano concertos, string quartets and piano trios, violin and cello sonatas, and many more kinds of chamber music; there are piano sonatas and numerous sets of variations for piano as well as oratorios, an opera, Masses, arias and songs – not to mention a host of lesser compositions. The number of major works among them indicates however that Beethoven was a very different sort of composer from Mozart and Haydn. There is only one opera

ABOVE Beethoven lived in several different houses during his life in Vienna, as well as migrating to villages near the city such as Heiligenstadt and Grinzing in the summer. This is no. 2 Pfarrplatz, Grinzing, now a suburb of Vienna.

LEFT Part of the manuscript of the last movement of Beethoven's Ninth Symphony in D minor, Opus 125, composed in 1822–4.

and one violin concerto, there are two Masses, five piano concertos, and nine symphonies. Compare this with Mozart's fifty symphonies and Haydn's hundred, for example. In spite of the fact that throughout his life Beethoven found composition far from easy, the sheer scope and size of his individual works is beyond anything that had been seen hitherto in the history of music. In this respect Beethoven opened up the Romantic vista: he felt that he needed time and space in which to say what was in his musical mind. And he handed on his new achievements to his successors, though in the hands of less talented men his gift was often abused, and ultimately devalued.

What also points to the Romantic rather than the Classical aesthetic in Beethoven is that, more than any previous composer, his music was the direct outpouring of its creator. We see in it the reflection of the nature of the man himself. He had at best a difficult life, since he did not find relationships easy to form or to sustain, and his affliction of deafness made him suspicious, and therefore put intolerable strains on the relationships that he was able to form. One of the saddest, and yet most eloquent comments on the entire problem of his personality in relation to his music was the document that he got Schindler to draw up for Schuppanzigh and the other members of the ensemble to sign, promising that they would all do their best, and strive together for excellence during the first performance that they were to give of the Opus 127 quartet. It is hard to imagine either Mozart or Haydn ever dreaming of such an expedient, and through it we share the agony of Beethoven himself.

From a purely technical viewpoint the onset of deafness is a disturbing but not a catastrophic event for a composer, because he is able to hear the sounds in his head as or before he writes them down. It happened to Handel's contemporary Mattheson, and subsequently to Fauré. In Beethoven's case there was the problem that some of his music was so advanced for its day that people who knew that he was deaf would say that he wrote nonsense. It was for this reason that he tried to keep it a secret for so long. However, as far as the actual effect that his deafness had on his music is concerned, we can only speculate. Had he been able to hear what his contemporaries were writing later in his career, then it is conceivable that he might have written somewhat differently himself. By the same token, however, had he been able to hear the rich sonorities of a modern grand piano, he might well not have written some of the thick textures that appear in some of his piano music. Of much more concern is the actual content of the music; possibly his mode of expression in the final quartets would not have been so intimate, so intense, as he withdrew more and more into his inner world, had his hearing not been affected, and whatever the cost to Beethoven himself, perhaps that is something for which music lovers should be thankful.

Of course other composers have had difficult lives – Mozart's, for example, was far from easy – but they were always able to make the

Beethoven's last study in the Schwarzspanierhaus in Vienna, where he died. It was sketched a few days after his death in 1827 by Johann Nepomuk Hoechle.

music exist independently, it seemed. No one who has ever read Beethoven's heart-rending letters known as the *Heiligenstadt Testament* and *To the Immortal Beloved* can ever forget them as they listen to his music. The music is, beyond any shadow of doubt, the man. One might add in parenthesis that just as there were less admirable aspects to the man, so there are also, on occasion, to the music. In Beethoven's case, however, even those may be seen as a direct outcome of his grapplings with expression, and never simply laziness or carelessness. The music wells up from an inner force or daemonic energy, and one feels that Beethoven could not have ignored that force even if he had wanted to, especially since at times the act of composition was more like a wrestling match, as Schindler recorded when he went to visit Beethoven during the composition of the *Missa solemnis* in 1819. As the composer emerged from the room in which he had been struggling with the fugue in the Credo of the Mass, Schindler reported that he looked as if he had been fighting with a whole army of contrapuntalists.

Beethoven was wrestling not only with the more difficult problems of composition, but with the problems of the creative artist in the modern world, and ultimately with some of the problems of man's very existence. One would expect such a programme to be carried out on a colossal scale, and indeed it was. The fact that Beethoven speaks to each generation anew – as does Shakespeare – is witness to the relevance of what he had to say, and to its enduring quality, though different aspects speak to different epochs. It is the works of his middle period that appeal to the widest audience, and those who are devotees of the Ninth Symphony may well not regard the slow movement of the A minor quartet, Opus 132, in quite the same way. But the point is that he has something to say to everyone, and as E. M. Forster pointed out in *Howards End*, it is because he shows us the darker side of our existence that we trust him in other areas. Patently this is very different music from most of what had been produced before, and the very fact that we can use terms such as 'meaning' shows just how different. At the same time it is a regrettable fact – because meaning has, by implication, understanding as its complement – that a conviction that some people are unable to 'understand' some music means that they do not, therefore, truly appreciate Classical music, and are thus deterred from sharing in its delights.

From a specifically technical point of view, Beethoven has also left musicians on the horns of a dilemma. His implicit explosion of forms and tonality paved the way for a schism in Western music that is unlikely to be healed for a very long time, if at all. Indeed, since his influence on tonality has only become fully clear to us in the twentieth century, we are still absorbing its effects. Either way, one may say without fear of contradiction that after Beethoven things could never be the same again. In the wake of that explosion, we shall consider first his successors in the symphonic tradition.

5. Romanticism

A ball at the Paris Opéra in the aftermath of the French Revolution highlights the fact that the departure of the old order was not only a political and historical event but an artistic one too. Henceforth a new breath was to blow through music, not only in France but also throughout Western Europe.

OVERLEAF Franz Peter Schubert (1797–1828) at the piano, surrounded by some of his Viennese friends, notably Spaun and Bauernfeld, Vogl, Schwind and Grillparzer, and his sister Fröhlich.

Lieder and religious music

Among those who carried torches at Beethoven's funeral in 1827 was Franz Peter Schubert, born in 1797. Like Beethoven he wrote nine symphonies, but unlike him he enjoyed no international reputation during his lifetime. Schubert wrote piano sonatas and chamber music, but the preponderance of vocal music – six Masses, seventeen operatic works and more than six hundred *Lieder* – shows that he had a particular affinity with the human voice, and with melody in general. This was, of course, the golden age of the *Lied*, and there was a succession of exponents in the nineteenth century of what had become a highly developed art form, one notable example being Robert Schumann (1810–56), also remarkable for his great melodic gifts, though perhaps with less spontaneity than Schubert. The piano accompaniments to their *Lieder* are extremely interesting, and show how quickly the potential of the relatively new instrument was being exploited, and how quickly it established itself as the ideal vehicle for accompanying these songs. If Schubert provided a rich harmonic sense, with wide variety and ingenious touches in his accompaniments, Schumann made the piano and the voice almost equal partners in the overall concept. Johannes Brahms (1833–97) was the next great *Lieder* writer, though in spirit he looked back to Schubert rather than to Schumann. Perhaps the work of all three men was synthesized in the songs of Hugo Wolf (1860–1903), for after him there was no further significant development in the art.

Turning to the other main area of non-operatic vocal writing – part-songs and cantatas, Church music and oratorio – it is much less easy to discern any continuous stream of artistic development. There was certainly a call for part-songs, largely in response to a rise of nationalistic feeling and interest in folksong, which had never been lacking among German composers in particular. The first half of the nineteenth century saw the inauguration of music festivals and the setting up of choral societies. Schubert and Schumann both wrote for this new field, as did Mendelssohn, Liszt and Gounod, though much

Robert Schumann (1810–56) as a young man: a lithograph after Menzel.

of it has been deservedly forgotten, and only items such as Brahms' *Alto Rhapsody* have found their way into the permanent repertoire and become known to the general public.

In the sphere of Church music the situation was even bleaker. Schubert in Vienna and Cherubini in Paris were producing the best Catholic Church music in the early part of the century, but though musically accomplished, it is hardly likely to inspire with devotional fervour. Although an attempt had been made to produce music suited to a concept of what was correct and proper for worship, it ended by being neither religious nor secular. The same is true of Gounod's devotional music, and even the Abbé Liszt was unable to do better. The best of Rossini and Verdi in this field – particularly Verdi's *Requiem* – is highly emotionally charged, but not necessarily with religious motivation. The achievement of Berlioz in his *Grande Messe des Morts* and *Te Deum* is similarly exciting and interesting, but it is

RIGHT Hector Berlioz (1803–69) in a lithograph by Preuzhofer dated 1845.

BELOW Hugo Wolf (1860–1903) in 1889, shortly after the death of his father, when he was living in Vienna and experiencing financial hardship.

OVERLEAF The artist Josef Danhauser (1805–45) gave pride of place to Beethoven in this painting of 1840. He made the bust of Beethoven from a death-mask and drawings of the composer on his death-bed, and it presides here over Liszt at the piano. The other distinguished members of the company are Dumas, Berlioz, George Sand, Paganini, Rossini and the Countess d'Agoult.

principally symphonic music on a religious text. It was not until Anton Bruckner (1824–96) came on the scene that one finds a convincing idiom that was inspired and devotional, and yet at the same time did not compromise his artistic integrity. Samuel Sebastian Wesley (1810–76) marked an important stage in the revival of the Anglican Church's music, which was to enjoy a period of continued development and bring considerable advantages to the musical life of the nation for many years to come.

The one item of choral music that undoubtedly flourished was the oratorio – especially in England and Germany. It is a wide field, to say the least, and ranges from Spohr's neglected *The Last Judgment* (1826) and Mendelssohn's *St Paul* (1836) and *Elijah* (1846), to Liszt's *Christus* (1856) and *Legend of St Elizabeth* (1857–62), Franck's *Béatitudes* (1879), Gounod's *Rédemption* (1882) and *Mors et vita* (1885). As ever, Berlioz stands somewhat apart with his *L'Enfance du Christ* (1854), as does Brahms with his *German Requiem* (1868); the latter is not strictly speaking an oratorio – even amongst such a heterogeneous collection – but nor on the other hand is it liturgical, since it includes no Latin at all, let alone the text of the Requiem Mass, but is rather a setting of Biblical texts in German.

Instrumental music in the Romantic age

When we turn to the instrumental music of the period (apart from orchestral music, that is) we encounter the same great names – Schubert, Schumann and Brahms, the first two especially significant for their piano quintets, and Brahms for his clarinet quintet; in the realm of piano music alone they stand out as having enriched the repertoire with some magnificent compositions. Despite the fact that they carry us well into the Romantic era, all three have marked Classical tendencies in the overall spirit of their music, if not in any particular details. Indeed, their music provides a large amount of what is known today as the classical repertoire with a small 'c'. Such terms may confuse more than clarify, so for the last form to be considered in this section – the symphony – rather than follow the two main trends individually, it is simpler to chart its progress through the rest of the century chronologically. Both trends emanated from Beethoven.

The evolution of the symphony

If we return to Schubert, we find that of his nine symphonies two are particularly important – the *Unfinished* (1822) and the C major (1828), usually known as *The Great*. His melodic sense and harmonic interest are present in these large-scale works as well as in more intimate ones, but in his symphonies he also reveals his love of varied orchestration – the colour and texture made possible by the interplay of the instruments themselves. Schubert did not simply translate his music to an orchestral dimension; it was conceived in orchestral terms from the outset. This fact, and its melodic content, prevent the length and repetition of the great C major from becoming tedious; but in its day the instrumental technique demanded by the composer, especially from the wind section, made it seem extremely difficult.

On the whole Schumann was a much less accomplished orchestral writer than Schubert, at least as far as orchestration itself was concerned, but his symphonic writing has a spontaneity and energy, and also a programmatic (or descriptive) element, that smacks of Mendelssohn. Another link with the latter is the fact that the D minor symphony (in the 1851 version) was written as one consecutive piece of music, though still having four distinguishable movements, which shows that fairly soon after its elaboration at Beethoven's hands the symphony went through yet another period of experimentation.

The term 'programmatic element' was used above in relation to Schumann and, by implication, also to Mendelssohn. It was used advisedly, for in applying it to a musical work there is a danger of being blinded to other elements. In fact Mendelssohn's two chief symphonies, the *Italian* (1833) and the *Scottish* (1842) are really more pictorial than programmatic, and landscape music is perhaps a better term for them than programme music. This also applies to Mendelssohn's overtures such as *The Hebrides (Fingal's Cave*, 1832), *Calm Sea and Prosperous Voyage* (1828–32) and *Melusine* (1833). Since the overture to *A Midsummer Night's Dream* was composed as part of the incidental music to the play, it is inevitable that it should include a certain programmatic element. In all these symphonies and overtures, however, there is a feeling of Classicism in the control and balance, and even in the form since most of the overtures are in sonata form. In any case, if one compares them with Mendelssohn's violin concerto, where there is no hint of the programmatic element, one sees that musically they are very similar indeed. Romantic they certainly are, but in some very positive respects they are nonetheless Classical too.

By contrast, Berlioz' *Symphonie fantastique* (1830) is a supremely programmatic work, since the descriptive element deliberately infuses the whole work. In adding a fifth movement Berlioz was using the form devised by Beethoven for his Sixth Symphony, which was also his most programmatic – as its popular name, the *Pastoral*, indicates. Berlioz was not breaking new ground in this respect, therefore, but he certainly did in his orchestration, even if some of the effects are more interesting in theory than in actual performance, such as the flute and trombone chords in the *Grande Messe des Morts*, for which one has to listen very carefully. The next symphony, *Harold in Italy* (1834), is more a viola concerto than a symphony, though it demonstrated that Berlioz was capable of producing very beautiful orchestration in an intimate as well as a grand manner. Both this and his dramatic symphony *Romeo and Juliet* (1839) show how fluid the concept of the symphony had become by this time and also,

Felix Mendelssohn (1809–47) at the age of twenty-one, during his visit to Rome in 1831.

incidentally, that at the most intense moments in the story or programme – the love and death scenes – Berlioz felt the need to shake off the shackles of words and resort to the greater freedom of solely instrumental music.

Berlioz was for a long time a much misunderstood composer, and it was certainly easy to make fun of him. Also, some of his effects – despite the grandeur of the conception – are not as impressive in practice as they are on paper. At best, however, there was a Beethoven-like drive in his restless creative urge, and he handed on some important gifts to his successors, not least his pioneering of modern conducting technique. It is significant that Liszt's *Faust* symphony (1854) was dedicated to Berlioz, for one sees in it, and indeed in Liszt's other symphonies and symphonic poems, features that closely resemble the work of Berlioz, and yet at the same time the characteristics that make so much of Liszt's orchestral music unpalatable to contemporary ears. The rhetoric and theatrical gesture are too flamboyant, too grandiose for the musical substance that has to support them. One sees Liszt's influence in the César

The keyboard as battlefield. General Bass does battle with Liszt in an amusing anonymous lithograph dating from 1842.

Der General Bass wird durch List in seinen festen Linien überrumpelt u. überwunden.

ABOVE Johann Strauss II (1825–99), as depicted in a silhouette by Hans Schliessmann.

LEFT Although essentially a composer of light music, Johann Strauss enjoyed the friendship of Brahms, with whom he is seen on the verandah at Bad Ischl.

The title page of *An der schönen blauen Donau* (the Blue Danube waltz), Opus 314, which Johann Strauss composed in 1867.

Franck symphony of 1888; it remains an individual work, and is not programmatic by any means, but it may be regarded as the end of that particular line of development.

After following one path to its end, to return to the four symphonies of Brahms is to feel once more the breadth of Classicism. Brahms was no less faithfully following the tradition of Beethoven than were Berlioz and Liszt, but his control, self-criticism and application set him apart from them, for despite the Classical aspects of his symphonies, who could deny that the melody, the harmony, and above all the orchestration deployed by Brahms are sheer Romanticism. Much the same may be said of his overtures – the *Tragic* and the *Academic Festival* – and his concertos – violin, violin and cello, and the two for piano. In the case of the piano concertos, especially the second, the form is closer to a piano symphony than a concerto, but to some extent this is true of all his concertos.

The same overall Classical feeling – when contrasted with Berlioz and Liszt – emanates from Bruckner's symphonies, though at the same time his colossal conceptions deserve to be regarded as the apotheosis of the Romantic symphony. As in Bruckner's choral music, it is the dedication of the man behind the music that shines through his work, and those who have glibly pronounced about his indebtedness to Wagner overlook much that is more worthy of mention.

It is odd that Bruckner and Mahler should, in the last fifteen or twenty years, have found the wide public that was denied them earlier, and that the former should represent a summing-up of the

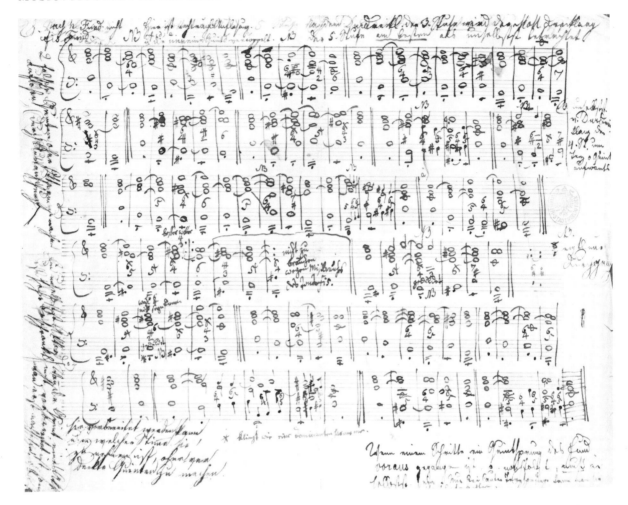

more Classical element in the symphonic evolution, whereas the latter seems to stand for the Romantic-programmatic development. A consideration of Mahler must be deferred to a later chapter, for not only was he later in time, but he foreshadowed the last great development in Western music to date, which was set in motion by the trio of Schönberg, Berg and Webern with their totally new concept of composition.

Before leaving symphonic development, however, reference must be made to Tchaikovsky and Dvorak, for although they will be referred to later in connection with nationalistic tendencies, it is at the same time impossible to divorce them from the main stream of symphonic development in the Romantic mould, which means in effect the German or Germanic tradition. Much the same may be said of their concertos as was said about those of Brahms concerning proximity to symphonic forms – especially Tchaikovsky's violin concerto (1878) and first piano concerto (1875), and Dvorak's cello concerto (1895). Temperamentally, however, one feels that

Anton Bruckner (1824–96) was engaged in an arduous study of harmony and counterpoint between 1857 and 1861 with the well-known teacher Simon Sechter. Like any other student, his work was presented for criticism, as we see from this example.

ABOVE Antonin Dvorak
(1841–1904).

RIGHT Piotr Ilitch
Tchaikovsky (1840–93),
seen here in the robes of a
Doctor of Music of
Cambridge, an honorary
degree conferred on him
in the last year of his life.

Tchaikovsky leaned more towards the Berlioz-Liszt tradition than towards Brahms and Bruckner. With Dvorak, on the other hand, the opposite was true, and it is easy to see an affinity with Brahms, especially in his treatment of orchestration and melody. A predilection for folk melodies was common to both composers: in his Ninth Symphony (*From the New World*, 1893), Dvorak, the Bohemian, achieved a remarkable feat in taking American Indian melodies and Negro spirituals and binding them into what has become one of the most popular symphonies of all.

The great age of opera

Nowadays we tend to think of grand opera as something of Italian origin, largely because so many opera composers, and singers too, have been Italian. In fact it was France, and Paris in particular, from which it came. There are two very good reasons for this: firstly, after the Revolution of 1789 and the establishment of the Napoleonic Empire, Paris became virtually the centre of Europe; secondly, opera had a musical ancestor in France in the form of the spectacle that had been codified by Lully, and then reformed to a certain extent by Gluck. Paris became the operatic capital of Europe during the first half of the nineteenth century, and Verdi, writing in 1851, referred to '... the most expensive singers, the largest ballet corps in the world, and an orchestra without equal for its strength and distinction, accompanying unending masses of chorus singers'. Such was the Paris Opéra, and it was to be complemented by the most opulent opera house in the world when Garnier started to build his 'palace', as it is still known, in 1862.

What had started out as essentially an aristocratic entertainment had now become 'democratized', for we must remember that grand opera was the most popular form of entertainment – even mass entertainment – in Paris at the time. When Gasparo Spontini (1774–1851), the Empress Josephine's favourite composer, had his *La Vestale* produced there in 1807 he doubtless thought that he was being faithful to the spirit of Gluck; in fact he had initiated the new grand opera, even though it would take another twenty or so years for it to blossom. Other opera composers were also working in Paris at this time, notably Cherubini – Napoleon's favourite – and Etienne-Nicolas Méhul (1763–1817), but the collapse of Napoleon and the subsequent upheaval meant that it was not until the Bourbon restoration that the artistic climate settled down once more.

The grand opera style became firmly established in France with the triumvirate of Louis Véron (1798–1867), director of the Opéra, the librettist Eugène Scribe (1791–1861), and the composer Giacomo Meyerbeer (1791–1864) who, despite his name, was born Jakob Liebmann Beer in Berlin. Such are the ironies of fate that Meyerbeer went to Vienna to consult Salieri – Mozart's rival and at one time a teacher of Beethoven – who advised him to go to Italy. While he was

Jacques Offenbach (1819–80) was born in Cologne, the son of a Jewish cantor, but went to Paris at the age of fourteen, married there, and became a naturalized Frenchman in 1860.

Offenbach in a cartoon by Gill in November 1866; by then such successes as *Les deux Aveugles*, *La Belle Hélène* and *Barkouf* were behind him, and with *Barbe-Bleue* he had embarked that year on his greatest works.

there, Meyerbeer had a resounding success at La Fenice in Venice with *Il Crociato in Egitto* in 1824, and returned to Paris in triumph. The year before, also in Venice, Gioacchino Rossini (1792–1868) had had a failure with his serious opera *Semiramide*, and he too settled in Paris, where five years later, in 1829, he produced his grand opera *Guillaume Tell*. We tend to think of him primarily as a composer of comic opera, but it is interesting that with his last work he should have contributed so much to the world of grand opera.

The year before *Guillaume Tell*, in 1828, Daniel Auber (1782–1871) had produced his *La Muette de Portici* – also known as *Masaniello* – so Rossini's grand opera was not the first of its kind, but it happens to be one of the best. After that Meyerbeer embarked on a triumphal series of operas, among them *Le Prophète* (1849) and *L'Africaine*, first performed the year after his death in 1865. Probably the only other notable work of this period, on a par with *Guillaume Tell*, was *La Juive* (1835) by Jacques Fromental Halévy (1799–1862). It is easy to see how French grand opera influenced Bellini and Verdi – and even Wagner, for his *Rienzi* was certainly a direct product of it. And we must bear in mind that whatever we might think of such operas today, a great many people with discriminating taste enjoyed them, and continued to do so for much of the century. It was left to the Frenchman, Berlioz, to redeem the situation with *Les Troyens*, composed between 1856 and 1858, though only the second part was given in Paris in 1863, and the first part not until 1890.

Paris at this time was not wholly given up to grand opera. Alongside it was *opéra comique*, which, unlike grand opera, had spoken dialogue, and although it had its shortcomings it was a much less pretentious and, therefore, more spontaneous genre. In 1858 Jacques Offenbach (1819–80) produced *Orphée aux Enfers* and *La Belle Hélène* (1864), a stream which can be traced to London with the Gilbert and Sullivan comic operas, and to Vienna with Johann Strauss the Younger's *Die Fledermaus* (1874).

Somewhere between grand opera and comic opera comes a lyric work such as *Mignon* (1866) by Ambroise Thomas (1811–96), and *Faust* (1859) by Gounod (1818–93). In fact in its original form *Faust* was a comic opera, with spoken dialogue, but Gounod subsequently revised it and added recitatives. Also in this category, and for the same reason, is *Carmen* (1875) by Georges Bizet (1838–75), which shows that the 'comic' epithet denoted spoken dialogue rather than humour, since there is scarcely any comedy in *Carmen*. Despite a certain streak of exoticism in the plot and its setting, *Carmen* was most significant for its realism, which was to become an important aspect of opera at the end of the century. No less exotic was *Samson et Dalila* (1877) by Camille Saint-Saëns (1835–1921), which in some respects looks back to Gounod, and yet in its theme, setting, and spectacular moments it also takes a glance in the direction of grand opera. At all events the genre was played out by that time. Perhaps, to take a couplet from one of Gilbert and Sullivan's truly comic operas, art really did stop short in the cultivated court of the Empress Josephine.

Rossini in a Gill cartoon of July 1867. He had finally returned to Paris in 1853, and died there in November of 1868.

We saw earlier how Rossini ended his operatic career after he settled in Paris in 1824, and in a way that was artistically fitting, because he had left his native country, where the concept of opera was very different. For one thing, the division between *opera seria* and *opera buffa* had survived in Italy until well into the nineteenth century, and opera was the focal point of the country's musical energies at that time – as indeed it has largely remained to the present day. Furthermore, given the Italian temperament, there was probably less room for Romanticism to progress there than anywhere else in Europe. Rossini wrote no fewer than thirty-two operas, as well as two oratorios, twelve cantatas, two symphonies and some other instrumental compositions. Some of his serious operas were successful – such as *Tancredi* (1813) and *Otello* (1816) – but his comic operas have stood the test of time better. Several are known to the music-lover only through their overtures, but others such as *La Cenerentola* (1817) and *Le Comte Ory* (1828) are in the repertoire of many companies, and of course *Il Barbiere di Siviglia* (1816) is one of the masterpieces of Italian comic opera.

Even more prolific than Rossini was Gaetano Donizetti (1797–1848), who also wrote both serious and comic operas. Of his serious operas *Lucia di Lammermoor* (1835) is probably the one that is most often performed outside Italy; on the whole his comic operas have proved more lasting, since they do not usually depend on having a suitable prima donna for a coloratura role. *L'Elisir d'Amore* (1832), *La Fille du Régiment* (1840) and *Don Pasquale* (1843) are all established favourites, the first and last being strictly speaking *opera buffa*, while the second is true comic opera. Artistically speaking, Donizetti's heir was Verdi, but chronologically the next great Italian opera composer was Vincenzo Bellini (1801–35). In his short life he wrote ten serious operas, of which the best known are *La Sonnambula* (1831), *Norma* (1831) and *I Puritani* (1835). He had a marvellous melodic sense, and by comparison with Donizetti a marked refinement of manner.

Giuseppe Verdi (1813–1901) wrote twenty-six operas over a span of some sixty years, and through his life and work, without propounding any great theories or making any dramatic gestures of reform or breaking with the past, he brought Italian opera to its point of supreme development. In fact he devoted himself almost entirely to Italian opera, for apart from a string quartet, some songs, some settings of sacred texts, and the *Requiem*, everything he wrote was for the stage. The *Requiem* was originally inspired by the death of Rossini, though the project was shelved, and it was the death of Manzoni in 1873 that was its immediate *raison d'être*; even though the spirit of the music is intensely devout, it is also highly operatic.

In common with Bellini, Verdi wrote basically serious operas, apart from *Falstaff* (1893) and an unsuccessful early work. He drew not only from the experience of Donizetti and Rossini, but also from Meyerbeer as far as harmony and orchestration were concerned. Even so, Verdi remained essentially Italian, and was indeed closely associated with the *Risorgimento* that brought unity and independence to Italy. For patriots the letters of his name meant [*Viva*] *Vittorio Emanuele, Re d'Italia* ([Long Live] Victor Emanuel, King of Italy), and *Viva Verdi* became a rallying call. So strong was Verdi's Italianism that one tends to overlook the fact that he drew inspiration from Romantic authors such as Schiller, Victor Hugo and Dumas *fils*. For *Macbeth* (1847, revised 1865) he drew on Shakespeare, and it was with two other Shakespeare plays that Verdi brought Italian opera – both serious and comic – to their heights with *Otello* (1887) and *Falstaff* (1893) respectively.

Otello introduced no new element into Verdi's writing, but it has a sense of cohesion and continuity that was to become even more pronounced in *Falstaff*. Of course it has its contrasts, such as the storm music and the calm of the 'Willow Song' and 'Ave Maria', but between these extremes the overall effect is one of control, even restraint, and a unity that seems to have its roots in Verdi's response to Shakespeare's treatment of the story. The tragedy is essentially one of human failing, for it concerns our tendency so often to destroy the thing we love, and in so doing to kill part of ourselves. *Otello*'s

Vincenzo Bellini (1801–35) went to Paris in 1833, where he met Rossini, Chopin, Cherubini, Liszt and Heine and had a triumph with *I Puritani* in January 1835, but sadly he died later that year.

ABOVE Carl Maria von
Weber (1786–1826)
managed in his short
career to establish a truly
German opera. He died in
London and his spiritual
heir and successor in
Dresden, Richard
Wagner, delivered an
address over his grave
when his body was
returned to Germany
eighteen years later.

greatness, therefore, lies not in that it offers escape into a world of
romanticism, but that it shows each of us that we are responsible for
our own deeds. To convey this, Verdi took the age-old lyrical
tradition of his native land and elevated it to probably its highest and
most eloquent point.

Falstaff was Verdi's first successful comic opera, written in extreme
old age, almost as a final comment on life from someone who had lived
long and knew it well. It looks back, in musical and historical terms,
to the *opera buffa* tradition, but with considerable reservations, as one
might expect. There are, for example, no arias, apart from Fenton's
love song, and the opera is 'through-composed' which, as the term
suggests, means that there are virtually no breaks between sections,
and that it moves along at a cracking pace, speeding to the climaxes of
the endings of the second and third acts. Through-composition also
helps to give great flexibility in the changes of mood, so that the
overall impression is one of a kaleidoscope, where the same elements
are ever-present, but the subtle turning of the apparatus brings a
seemingly endless succession of new effects. The opera ends with a
fugue to the words 'all the world's a joke', which is both a summing
up of the whole tradition of the *buffo* ensemble, and at the same time a
statement about life itself. In some ways it may be regarded, too, as an
adjustment to the essentially tragic vision of life as seen in *Otello*,
though by no means negating it.

Before leaving nineteenth-century opera we must turn to
Germany, to Carl Maria von Weber (1786–1826). After studying
with Michael Haydn and Abt Vogler, Weber became director of the
Prague Opera in 1813, and of the Dresden Opera three years later.
His three chief works are *Der Freischütz* (1821), *Euryanthe* (1832)
and *Oberon* (1826). Weber established German Romantic opera with,
in particular, *Der Freischütz*. With *Euryanthe*, which is almost on the
scale of grand opera, he prefigured Richard Wagner (1813–83) with
certain effects, such as unbroken music and contrasting harmonies to
emphasize the diverse forces at work, as well as the use of musical
themes that recur and are transformed. There was a comparable
trend in symphonic writing and the cyclical principle as used by Liszt
and Franck, for example, but it was a new element in opera, and one
that Wagner took to its limit.

Cyclicism, or the cyclical principle, sounds more complex than in
fact it is, especially if one bears in mind its literary application to a
cycle of poems or stories forming a continuous narrative around a
central event or period of history. In music the central event is a
theme, or possibly several themes, which are developed in such a way
that they connect the various movements of a composition and give it
unity of musical thought. Throughout musical history one of the
recurring problems has been how to achieve extended composition,
and variety of texture generally, without losing overall unity. It is not
hard to see the appeal of the cyclical principle, then, for it offers a
fundamental unity in the repetition of a theme, much as the ear will

LEFT Verdi, towards the
end of his life, with the
tenor Francesco
Tamagno, creator of the
role of Otello,
photographed at
Montecatini in Italy.

Richard Wagner
(1813–83).

pick up the rhymes in poetry. It also means that several themes may
be introduced and kept alive simultaneously; a kind of musical
subconscious is created, from which themes may be drawn from time
to time if the composer wishes to place particular emphasis on them,
and then returned to the overall texture. The appeal of such a concept
was of immense significance for the evolution of Wagner's operatic
style, especially in *The Ring*.

Wagner is one of the gigantic figures not only in opera but in the
whole of music, and in common with Verdi he wrote almost entirely
for the theatre. Indeed there is a further parallel, since Wagner
brought German Romantic opera to a summit of perfection much as
Verdi had done for Italian opera. But Wagner went beyond Verdi, or

Wagner and Cosima, with Liszt and Hans von Wolzogen, in Wagner's study at Villa Wahnfried at Bayreuth. A woodcut of the oil painting by Beckmann.

at least he articulated his ideas more freely. He believed that the purpose of music was to further dramatic expression, and so he created a new form of music drama. We know almost as much about Wagner the man as we do about Beethoven, but whereas with Beethoven our knowledge is acquired almost independently of his music, in Wagner's case it is carefully presented to us in a very self-conscious manner.

One may like or dislike both the man and his music, but for his twofold achievement in German opera and the creation of music drama he is undeniably an important figure. For us in the twentieth century he has a third claim to fame. In his last works he carried harmonic development to the point where Classical tonality dissolved and Romantic influences triumphed. Only with Wagner can we see the true culmination of 'the Classical style', and we live today with the implications of his work.

His first success was with a grand opera of the traditional sort, *Rienzi*, in Dresden in 1842, and the following year he produced *Der Fliegende Holländer*, which is more in the tradition of Weber; as a result of the success of these two operas he was appointed director of the Dresden Opera, again following in Weber's footsteps. The next opera, *Tannhäuser* (1845), also for Dresden, was in some respects a

187

LEFT A silhouette by Böhler in which the critic Eduard Hanslich teaches Wagner how to compose.

RIGHT The death of Siegmund from Wagner's opera *Die Walküre* at Bayreuth, drawn by Kurt Etwatt.

BELOW Wagner's poetic vision had to have a practical realization on the stage. Here the Rhine Maidens are seen with mechanical aids to swimming.

return to grand opera, though in fact it looked forward to *Lohengrin* (1850) and to *The Ring* cycle. There was political trouble in Germany as elsewhere in Europe in 1848, and Wagner decided to go and live in Switzerland, where he remained for the next ten years. He committed his thoughts on opera to paper, and wrote the poems that became the libretto for the four dramas known as *Der Ring des Nibelungen*. *Das Rheingold* and *Die Walküre* were ready by 1857, together with part of *Siegfried*, but it was not until 1874 that the last part, *Götterdämmerung*, was finished, paving the way for the first complete performance of the cycle two years later in the specially built theatre at Bayreuth. Other works had been completed in the meantime, notably *Tristan und Isolde* (1857–9) and *Die Meistersinger von Nürnberg* (1862–7), and his last opera *Parsifal* (1882).

It was *The Ring* above all that illustrated Wagner's use of musical themes or *leitmotifs*, not only as a means of introducing characters, but abstract ideas too, such as fate, renunciation or redemption. These themes are not superimposed on the harmonic texture, as a melody might be sung with accompaniment, but provide the musical fibre from which the entire drama is spun. Orchestra and singers are one in their exploration and expression of the themes, while setting, plot and character all work together in total synthesis.

Die Meistersinger showed that Wagner had not totally forgotten Romantic opera, or even grand opera for that matter, but *Tristan* shows most clearly the harmonic features that may be traced through Bruckner, Mahler and Richard Strauss to Schönberg, Berg and Webern. There is no doubt that Wagner's influence was enormous and omnipresent, though it is also true to say that many composers tried to resist it, and for a long time it seemed as if Romanticism and post-Romanticism, as seen in the work of Hugo Wolf (1860–1903), Gustav Mahler (1860–1911) and Richard Strauss (1864–1949), had carried the day. This was supported by the historical development of the rise of the new German Empire after 1871 and the tide of events leading up to the outbreak of World War One, which makes 1914 the real turning-point rather than 1900. Nevertheless there were two forces challenging German superiority in music. The first was a renaissance in native French music, and the second was the much wider tide of nationalism which had been rising throughout the previous century.

The influence of nationalism

The Classical style in music actually began with the last echoes of the Baroque as it merged into Rococo, and no sooner had it reached the peak of its development into Classicism than it turned to Romanticism. All these labels, however, only mark the emergence of a style, and have been added with the benefit of hindsight; as ever, there were times when several tendencies were visible at any one moment, and even composers who were similar in some respects showed quite different characteristics in others.

Since the initiative in music had passed to Germany, as Romanticism developed it became almost totally identified with German music, and it was this that became the accepted international style. Certainly Germany had plenty to offer at the time, for having already absorbed its own folk music and song it was well placed to take the lead. In fact folk music has played a much smaller part in the development of national schools of music, certainly from the purely technical viewpoint, than is often thought, though certain idioms and forms have always carried strong national associations. Nevertheless an awakening of nationalism took place during the nineteenth century, both politically and artistically, and there is a temptation to regard the whole phenomenon as part of the broader historical

LEFT *Fantaisie brillante* on Liszt – a somewhat cruel caricature on some of the more flamboyant aspects of the man and his career, and yet one that was by no means without foundation.

RIGHT A drawing by D. Maclise of Niccolò Paganini (1782–1840) at the King's Theatre, Haymarket, London. Paganini was the epitome of the Romantic virtuoso, and the almost supernatural aura he cultivated heightened his reputation to the point where, on arrival in London, he was reputed to have been followed by people curious to see whether he were truly flesh and blood. In any event, he made important contributions to the development of violin technique.

Jenny Lind (1820–87) was known as the 'Swedish Nightingale' for the purity of her soprano voice, which won her international acclaim. She is seen here in Donizetti's *Lucia di Lammermoor*.

process, turning around 1848, the year of revolution in Europe and the year of Marx' and Engels' *Communist Manifesto*. Yet those two aspects of 1848 show that there were two interlocking forces at work on the historical level – tendencies to both nationalism and internationalism, or even supranationalism. In fact in music the situation was not quite the same. The reaction against German-dominated Romanticism was only articulated much later in the century, particularly, towards the end of it, by the French. Earlier forms of nationalism had tended to arise not by way of protest but simply because the seeds of Romanticism had been sown, and happened to find good soil. In fact when one looks at the careers and musical personalities of musicians as markedly nationalistic as Chopin and Liszt, one sees that the characteristics that unite them as Romantics are much stronger than the national characteristics that would set them apart. Of course Liszt drew directly on Chopin's pianistic style, which is a very definite bond, and both were virtuosi of the instrument; together with Mendelssohn and Schumann, they can help to put the whole question of Romanticism and nationalism into perspective.

These four composers were born within a very short space of time: Mendelssohn in 1809, Chopin and Schumann in 1810, and Liszt in 1811. All were virtuoso pianists, and the first three all died relatively young: Mendelssohn in 1847, Chopin in 1849 and Schumann in 1856. Liszt survived until 1886, but his life was so colourful that, if he did not provide a picture of the brilliant young Romantic artist dying in his prime, he certainly made up for it in other ways. Together they provide a composite image of the Romantic musician *par excellence*, reaching its culmination in the flamboyant Liszt. It is no surprise that when Liszt met Paganini (1782–1840) in Paris, he fell under his spell, and was induced to try and do for the piano what Paganini had done for the violin; that aspect of the Romantic temperament – the showy virtuoso – could hardly have been taken to greater extremes.

When we consider the original four as individuals, however, we see what each of them brought to the main stream of music. Mendelssohn came from Hamburg in northern Germany, and represented the development of the mainly Protestant tradition. His oratorios found a firm place in the English choral repertoire, and indeed after Handel he was the foreign composer whom the English took most warmly to their hearts. Mendelssohn was also a great admirer of J.S. Bach, whose *St Matthew Passion* he revived in Berlin in 1829. One of the Romantics' great gifts to posterity was that they prepared the way for the rise of musicology. Schumann, too, was a great admirer of Bach, though Schumann came from the opposite end of Germany from Mendelssohn, and temperamentally stood midway between him and the other two in the group: Mendelssohn could be said to be conservative, Chopin and Liszt somewhat radical, and Schumann to display tendencies in both directions. His piano music is not easy to play, though he never indulged in bravura for its own sake. With Chopin and Liszt, on the other hand, we feel that their whole concern was to sweep us off our feet. Theirs was the technical virtuosity that one tends to associate with Romanticism, though in Chopin's case it was less marked than in Liszt's, and no doubt less marked than subsequent performers of Chopin's music have tended to convey. Chopin, too, studied Bach, especially during the time when he was composing the preludes, while Liszt celebrated his debt to Bach by writing a fugue on his name – a somewhat idiosyncratic demonstration.

It is almost impossible to think of Chopin without thinking of Poland, and yet he lived in Paris from 1831 onwards, and although he exploited the forms of the mazurka and the polonaise, he rarely quoted directly from Polish folk music. It was the idiom rather than the direct use of, or even reference to, folk music that gives his work its nationalistic flavour. In fact the polonaise as a form had been used by Bach much earlier, and Chopin's importance from a specifically musical point of view is his development of piano technique and harmonic sense, and of forms such as the *étude* and the *ballade*. By comparison with this, therefore, his significance as a nationalistic composer is of comparatively minor concern, certainly outside Poland.

Much the same could be said of Liszt, and indeed in his case one sees not only a truly cosmopolitan figure, despite his Hungarian origins, but also a very eclectic composer. He certainly drew on his Hungarian background for musical inspiration, but perhaps more

OVERLEAF Louis Antoine Jullien (1812–60) ran a very successful series of Promenade concerts in London between 1838 and 1859, and did much to establish the role of the conductor as a personality and an interpreter of music. Despite the fact that he was reputed to have made large sums of money, he died in poverty and insanity.

Nikolas Rimsky-Korsakov (1844–1908).

relevant to his overall musical personality was the temperament that it gave him. Much of the fire, the dynamism and the impulsiveness in his music may be traced back to his origins, to which were added the initial German training that he had in Vienna and the influence of Romanticism at its height in Paris. He was in charge of music at the court of Weimar from 1848 to 1861, and for the next nine or ten years he lived in Rome, where he took holy orders. After that he spent most of his time in Rome, Weimar or Budapest. Rather like Chopin, however, Liszt's significance in the main stream of musical development depends on characteristics other than nationalism. The general overall picture of European music in the early nineteenth century was essentially a cosmopolitan one, with these early excursions into nationalism little more than an exotic dressing on the surface. It is true that there were certain aspects of music in France and Italy that one cannot dismiss so easily, but that was precisely because those two countries had well established traditions.

RIGHT Bedrich Smetana
(1824–84).

ABOVE Serge
Rachmaninov
(1873–1943).

When the new nationalism came, it was therefore more enduring
and more fundamental, and tended to occur in countries that had no
long or important traditions of their own, and had depended on other
countries, frequently Germany, for their music. This time it resulted
from a deliberate intent to break away, and an almost aggressive
determination to assert a national voice. The collection and
publishing of folksongs was one aspect of this, though apart from
using them as quotations in their music, the composers did not as a
rule incorporate them into their music to any great degree. Subjects
from national history might be used as libretti for operas, or to
provide patriotic associations to orchestral music, as, for example, in
Smetana's *Ma Vlast*. More important from the musical viewpoint,
however, was the way in which German music and its forms was
modified and transformed by elements taken from national idioms in
the spheres of form, harmony, tonality, melody and rhythm.

The first important school of national music to emerge was in

Russia. The music of the Orthodox Church had of course existed since earliest days, and had been enriched by later influences, but in the field of secular music Russia had, until the nineteenth century, depended chiefly on Italian, French and German composers and musicians. Naturally they, and the Russians they influenced, used folksong, but the first emergence of Russian music in its own right is usually taken to be the opera *A Life for the Tsar* (1836) by Michael Glinka (1804–57). He followed this with *Russlan and Ludmilla* (1842) – and the nationalist movement was launched. The chief composers were known as 'the mighty handful', and consisted of Mily Balakirev (1837–1910), Alexander Borodin (1833–87), Modest Mussorgsky (1839–81) and Nikolas Rimsky-Korsakov (1844–1908). It is interesting that all except Balakirev were amateurs, though Rimsky-Korsakov went on to teach Alexander Glazunov (1865–1936) and Igor Stravinsky (1882–1971).

Of course there were composers such as Anton Rubinstein (1829–94) who deliberately chose to remain Western in their music, and if they used national idiom it was in a very minor way. It is generally felt that this applied to Tchaikovsky (1840–93), for the most part, and even more so to Serge Rachmaninov (1873–1943). What had given 'the mighty handful' their impetus was the fact that they had had to create their idiom themselves. One never feels that a work such as Tchaikovsky's *Eugene Onegin* (1879), for example, is ever more than secondarily a Russian work, despite its setting; it belongs primarily in the cosmopolitan stream of opera. Another Russian composer who did not fall into the nationalistic category – but is equally hard to place in any other – was Alexander Scriabin (1872–1915). In the tradition rather of Chopin, Liszt and even Wagner, Scriabin is significant for his harmonic experiments that seemed to anticipate atonality.

In Czechoslovakia the situation was different, for as part of the Austrian Empire its musicians had not been isolated from the rest of Europe, and indeed had made some important contributions to the main stream of Western music. Nevertheless there was a distinct national stream, even if Czech composers did not feel impelled to distinguish it from Western music in general as the Russians had. Nationalism is apparent in the music of Anton Dvorak (1841–1904) and of the earlier Bedrich Smetana (1824–84). The most overtly nationalistic music is found in such works as Dvorak's *Slavonic Dances* and his late opera *Rusalka*, in Smetana's opera *The Bartered Bride* (1866) and his later symphonic poem *Ma Vlast*. A composer who made a conscious renunciation of Western styles after 1890 was Leos Janacek (1854–1928). It is interesting that his operatic works are today enjoying a greater international popularity than ever before.

After a trio of Czech composers in eastern Europe, we turn to a trio of Scandinavians in the north: Edvard Grieg (1843–1907) from Norway, Carl August Nielsen (1865–1931) from Denmark, and Jean

Sibelius (1865–1957) from Finland. Of the three, Grieg is perhaps the most demonstrably nationalistic, and Nielsen the least, with Sibelius somewhere in between the two. All of them studied for at least part of their youth in Germany, which shows how strong the pull of that country and its musical tradition was. We find the same phenomenon in American music, which was now beginning to emerge in its own right, but the first American composer of international note, Edward MacDowell (1861–1908), spent ten years studying and living in Germany, and there is little specifically American in his music. Not until Charles Ives (1874–1954) do we feel that a truly American composer has arrived on the scene, and it is no coincidence that, in common with the Russian 'mighty handful', Ives was not a professional – and therefore international – musician.

In England we find a similar situation, for although Edward Elgar (1857–1934) is thought of as a supremely English composer, it is hard to point to anything in his music that is specifically English, and it was certainly not influenced by folksong. If anything, one sees the hand of Wagner and certainly that of Brahms at work, especially in the use of *leitmotifs* from the former, and orchestration from the latter. Yet few composers have been more closely identified with the English national spirit than Elgar. In the purely musical as opposed to patriotic context, Elgar's significance lies more in the fact that he

Jean Sibelius
(1865–1957).

heralded a renaissance in English music – certainly it took on a much more nationalistic character after him – and he was the first English composer in more than two centuries to gain international status.

Something similar happened in Spain, where Felipe Pedrell (1841–1922) heralded a revival that took on more importance with Isaac Albéniz (1860–1909), in whose music Spanish nationalistic elements were clearly present, and with Manuel de Falla (1876–1946), though he also came under the influence of Debussy.

Before leaving nationalism in the late nineteenth century, however, it is appropriate to look at it in its widest context. For historical

Sir Edward Elgar (1857–1934), seen here in a recording studio with the cellist Beatrice Harrison on 15 November 1920.

reasons, as we have seen, and because genius is influenced by time and place and manifests itself in a variety of ways, nationalism in music varied greatly from country to country. Indeed, in many respects it was only in Russia that it had the fervently patriotic quality that the term nationalism implies. Composers with strong nationalistic tendencies – such as Grieg and Sibelius in Scandinavia, or Ives in America – left no disciples behind them, nor did they found any national schools to carry on their work. At the other end of the scale, composers such as Elgar or MacDowell gained a certain reputation as representatives of their respective countries simply because their talents were exceptional. The huge tide of international European music engulfed nationalism and swept it along in the main stream. At the same time that main stream was enriched in many ways by what nationalism had brought to it, and it is safe to say that without those contributions, the music of the twentieth century would have been considerably poorer. The one country to stand successfully against the tide had been France, and in so doing, France carried Western music into the twentieth century.

6. The Twentieth Century

French renaissance

It is customary to regard the resurgence of French music as dating from 1871, when the Franco-Prussian War ended and the Société Nationale de Musique was founded by, amongst others, Saint-Saëns, Franck, Lalo and Fauré. Their aim was to further the dissemination of contemporary French music. Of course Franck was only a Frenchman by adoption, being Belgian by birth, and of the four composers mentioned above he was the most cosmopolitan. Nevertheless he threw himself into the task, and in a remarkably short time they managed to get the works of young composers included in the programmes of public concerts given in Paris, which until then had been closed to them. Indeed one may see in Franck's championing of this cause an antidote to the claim that he was a kind of French Wagnerite, or at best a restrained Romantic, and indeed there is something positively anti-Romantic in the discipline, control and logic which are clearly evident in almost all of his music.

These qualities emerge in the work of his foremost pupil, Vincent d'Indy (1851–1931). D'Indy used a French folksong for his First Symphony (1886), but it was not through folksong that he came to be an important figure in French music. In fact in his opera *Fervaal* (1897) it is possible to detect traces of Wagner, but all the time a fundamental un-Romantic, even Classical quality underlies his music. Indeed, in 1894 d'Indy was one of the founders of the Schola Cantorum in Paris, where considerable emphasis was placed on early French music, and over a period of about thirty years he organized some two hundred concerts of music by Charpentier, Rameau, Gluck and Bach. In its day it was a powerful institution, and produced such diverse composers as Albert Roussel (1869–1937) and the strange but perhaps over-celebrated Erik Satie (1866–1925).

As far as symphonic composition was concerned, Franck gave the principle of cyclicism to French music, which d'Indy in his turn, and another pupil of Franck, Ernest Chausson (1855–99), also took up.

Fauré presiding at a session of the Société Musicale Indépendante, of which he became president in 1909. Standing behind Fauré, with his hands on the back of the chair, is the pianist and composer Louis Aubert (1877–1968) who, as a boy soprano, sang the *Pie Jesu* in the first performance of Fauré's *Requiem*. On Aubert's left is Maurice Ravel, André Caplat and the bearded Charles Koechlin. Next to Fauré at the keyboard is Roger-Ducasse, and the remaining members of the group are Mathot, Vuillermoz and Huré.

In fact d'Indy used the term '*forme cyclique*' in his *Cours de Composition* of 1909. Camille Saint-Saëns (1835–1921) also used cyclicism, as in his Third Symphony (1886), but it is for the medium of the piano concerto, however, that he deserves special mention. His First Piano Concerto (1858) was the first French essay in the form and, despite its evident debt to Liszt, was nevertheless a significant landmark in French music. In fact Saint-Saëns represented altogether a more truly French tradition than did Franck, and this emerges clearly in the work of his pupil Gabriel Fauré (1845–1924). It is less for his music, however, that Fauré has survived than for his personal and artistic integrity. He exemplified the French love of tradition and logic, and he tempered them with moderation and purity of musical form at a time when such things were far from popular in the musical world. Possibly Maurice Ravel (1875–1937) was his most famous pupil, but his influence has been carried into the world at large by the teaching of another of his pupils, Nadia Boulanger (1887–1979). It is highly significant that having been one of the founder members of the Société Nationale de Musique, in 1909 Fauré became president of the Société Musicale Indépendante, with Stravinsky and Bartók on its committee.

ABOVE The Paris Conservatoire moves house. A caricature of 1911 which portrays, amongst others, Fauré (director since 1905), Saint-Saëns, Massenet and Debussy.

After Franck and Saint–Saëns, the third great name in French music is Claude-Achille Debussy (1862–1918). Not only was he one of the greatest of French composers, but he was also one of the most important influences on twentieth-century music. Much has been made of the musical 'impressionism' of Debussy's work – the qualities it shares with Impressionist painting – but that is only part of its significance. Indeed, from a purely musical point of view Debussy's harmonic development was crucial for the future, though for what he contributed to piano technique alone he would deserve a place in musical history. In fact some of his later works are not at all impressionistic, and the string quartet of 1893 is classical in form and deals with themes cyclically. His orchestration could be termed impressionistic, perhaps, especially in *La Mer*, but far more important is the brilliance of Debussy's ear and musical imagination.

Similarly, those who enumerate the different influences discernible in the work of such diverse composers as Emmanuel Chabrier (1841–94), Wagner (with severe reservations), Mussorgsky, Grieg, Ravel, Chopin and Liszt, only tell a small part of the story. Debussy was first and foremost an individual; his conception of the role of music was fundamentally anti-Romantic, and he wanted to escape the all-enveloping superiority of German music.

Debussy came from a very modest family of Burgundian origin; his father was a marine, who had spent a great deal of time abroad before his marriage. Possibly he communicated to his son some of his enthusiasm for the places he had visited. Certainly few composers have evoked the sea with quite such devotion as Debussy, especially in *Sirènes* (1892–9), *La Mer* (1903–5) and certain passages of his opera *Pelléas et Mélisande* (1893–1902). During the Commune of 1871, Debussy's father was a captain in the revolutionary forces, and when they were defeated he was sent to prison for four years. Fortunately his parental role was taken over by a rich collector, Achille Arosa, who was able to ensure that in 1872 Debussy entered the Paris Conservatoire. He was later taken under the wing of Tchaikovsky's patroness Nadejda von Meck, and in 1884 won the Prix de Rome awarded by the French authorities for a two-year period of study in Rome.

Unfortunately Debussy's spell there was not at all productive, though two visits to Bayreuth made a great impression on him – on one occasion he was there at the same time as Gustav Mahler, Hugo Wolf and George Bernard Shaw. He exposed himself to a wide variety of musical experiences, from Palestrina to Javanese gamelan orchestras, before his musical imagination was finally liberated with the composition of *Pelléas*. There was, however, no brilliant future assured for him, and his emotional life was extremely fraught. His mistress between 1889 and 1899, Gabrielle Dupont, was driven to attempt suicide, and in 1904 he left his first wife, Rosalie Texier, who also tried to kill herself. In 1908 he married Emma Bardac, by whom he already had a daughter. Debussy's finances were no less difficult,

ABOVE A caricature of Camille Saint-Saëns (1835–1921) as a harpist.

205

LEFT Debussy's handwritten manuscript of *Prélude à l'Après-midi d'un Faune*, dated October 1899 and dedicated by the composer to his mistress Gabrielle Dupont. It was subsequently in the possession of the great pianist Cortot.

ABOVE Claude-Achille Debussy (1862–1918).

RIGHT Nijinsky, as portrayed by Bakst in Debussy's *Prélude à l'Après-midi d'un Faune*.

and he was obliged to travel extensively to conduct his works – which he did badly – in order to earn money. He also accepted commissions which diverted his energies from works of his own choosing. Cancer brought his sad life to an end in Paris in 1918, after the long, dark years of the war. As Nadia Boulanger wrote in the year after his death (though not specifically about him):

Now, we are going through an unprecedented period of transition, following the Wagnerian domination, a period that is perhaps so defined, so rich, because the willingly accepted yoke was imperious.

The vocabulary is therefore of necessity new, since the great creative souls are expressing a new state of mind; since they open our eyes to new visions, and since the artists who live in their effulgence use it as they do and, in these circumstances, abundance and originality are themselves part of the trouble we endure.

Unconsciously at that period she was preparing the way for the heartache of finding a new musical vocabulary in the wake of Debussy's effect on music, for even she could not have realized then just how agonizing that search was going to be for musicians. Nevertheless her conviction that music was a continuous stream, never at a standstill, made her accept all that has flowed since Debussy, in the realm of harmony in particular.

Of course Debussy did not immediately carry the day. One sees a counterbalance to the impressionistic trend in the work of Satie, though not by any means in direct opposition to Debussy, since they were to some extent colleagues. But if we follow the line through to Darius Milhaud and the other members of the group known as *Les Six* – Honneger, Poulenc, Durey, Auric and Tailleferre – on to André Jolivet and, finally, to Olivier Messiaen, we see how, slowly but increasingly, that stream moved away from Debussy. Even Ravel, despite several similarities in his use of orchestration, was distinctly more classical in outlook than Debussy, though perhaps this was a natural result of his proximity in musical temperament to his teacher Gabriel Fauré.

BELOW Arturo Toscanini (1867–1957) photographed during a recording of Debussy's *La Mer* on 4 March 1947.

Fauré's classicism or traditionalism was not a sterile influence in itself, however, and the gradual decay of French music through successive decades of this century should not be laid at his door. It was as if the French, in the effort of demonstrating that there was an alternative to Romanticism, had somehow exhausted their creative talent; thereafter they continued to be excellent musical educators and produce talented performers, but the muse had departed. As Gertrude Stein perceptively pointed out: 'Foreigners were not romantic to them [the French], they were just facts, nothing was sentimental they were just there, and strangely enough it did not make them make the art and literature of the twentieth century but it made them be the inevitable background for it.'

Italy and Germany

A similar situation existed in Italy, where tradition was carried on in the realm of opera. We saw earlier how *verismo* was creeping in at the end of the nineteenth century, and it was at its height in such operas as *Cavalleria Rusticana* (1890) by Pietro Mascagni (1863–1945), *I Pagliacci* (1892) by Ruggiero Leoncavallo (1858–1919), and *Tosca* (1900) by Giacomo Puccini (1858–1924). In fact the operas of Puccini show how late the spirit of Romanticism – or perhaps by this time it was post-Romanticism – survived in the hands of such a master.

As to the German tradition itself, we saw how *Lieder* were brought to a close with Hugo Wolf, and the orchestral tradition of Wagner and Liszt acquired even grander expression in the symphonies of Gustav Mahler (born in 1860, the same year as Hugo Wolf) and Richard Strauss. But in fact it was in a different direction that composers would find the way ahead, though Mahler's refinement of tonal language and its extension was to point to it. It was certainly a vital link in the chain that has brought us to the latter part of this century. Before turning to those enormous developments, however, we must look first at the progress of music in England, and then in America.

England

As was pointed out earlier, Elgar often appears to be the standard-bearer of English nationalism, when in fact what he really did was to mark the rebirth of English music. There were others of importance of course, notably C.H.H. Parry (1848–1918) and Charles Villiers Stanford (1852–1924) who were more or less his contemporaries. Both were teachers of the next great figure in English music, Ralph Vaughan Williams (1872–1958). Vaughan Williams was receptive to other influences, too, even to somewhat eclectic ones – notably Bach and Handel, Debussy and Ravel, English folksong and Tudor music – and yet he evolved a highly personal though profoundly English style, in a way that Elgar only partially achieved. Just how true this is may be appreciated by comparing Vaughan Williams' music with that of Gustav Holst (1874–1934), or Frederick Delius (1862–1934), for although their work has elements that are similar in feeling at times to that of Vaughan Williams, they remain fundamentally different. William Walton (b.1902) on the other hand, while writing in the traditional forms of symphony, concerto, opera and oratorio, is English only by association or in such a rarefied work as *Façade*. Walton was largely self-taught, and possibly as a result of this his music has a more cosmopolitan feel to it than that of almost any other English composer of this century. It is significant that if he is to be seen as the heir of any particular predecessor, then it should be of Elgar rather than Vaughan Williams.

ABOVE The blind Frederick Delius (1862–1934) by E. S. Proctor, listening to his *Mass of Life* in the Queen's Hall, London.

OVERLEAF Léon Bakst (1886–1925) arrived in Paris in 1908, where the ballet décors that he devised between 1910 and 1912 created a sensation and did much to revolutionize stage design. There is clear evidence of the impact of Eastern art on Bakst in the intensity and boldness of his use of colour, as for example in this set which he designed for Rimsky-Korsakov's *Shéhérazade*.

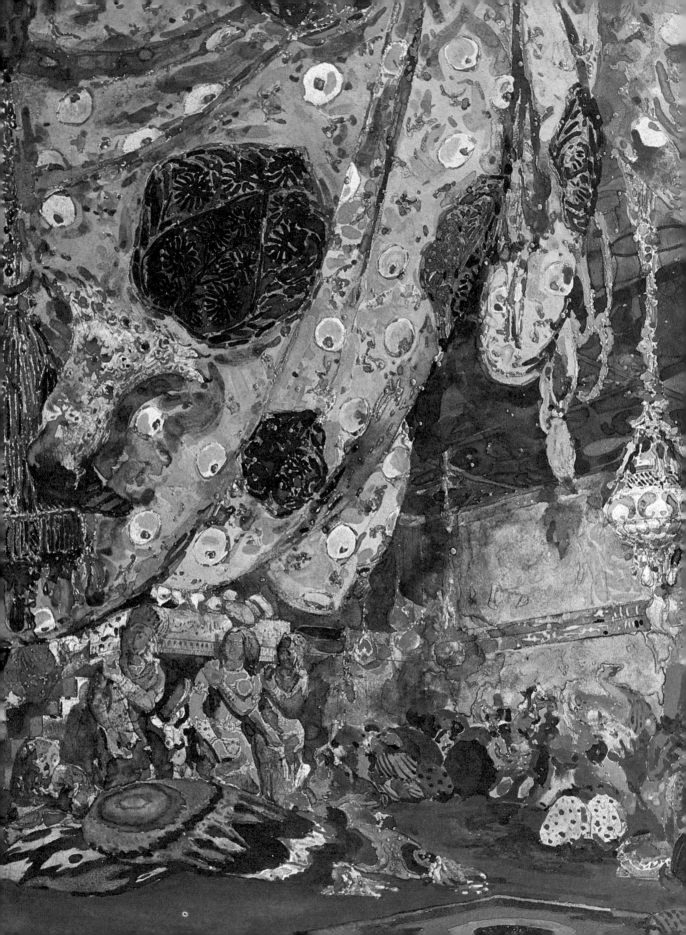

ABOVE Gustave Mahler
(1860–1911).

ABOVE Giacomo Puccini
(1858–1924).

LEFT Silhouettes by
Böhler of Mahler
conducting.

ABOVE Ralph Vaughan Williams (1872–1958), painted by Sir Gerald Kelly. The portrait, dated 1958–61, was given to the National Portrait Gallery, London, by the composer's widow.

OVERLEAF:
LEFT Edvard Grieg (1843–1907), painted by Erik Theodor Werenskjöld in 1892.

RIGHT Maurice Ravel (1875–1937) in a portrait by Ludwig Nauer.

America

In the early part of the twentieth century American composers still looked to Europe. Had he lived longer, George Gershwin (1898–1937) might have created a synthesis between 'popular' and 'classical' music; he approached Ravel for lessons but was turned down both by him and by Nadia Boulanger on the grounds that they would impair Gershwin's feeling for melody. Others actually did go and study in Paris, and retained their personalities more or less intact, producing music that was neither merely European-inspired nor specifically American in quality. Of these the most important are undoubtedly Aaron Copland (b.1900), Roy Harris (1898–1979) and Virgil Thomson (b.1896), all of whom studied with Boulanger. More or less of the same generation is Elliott Carter (b.1908).

Of course it is to America that the African slaves took their native melodies and dances, and above all their feeling for rhythm, which emerged as jazz towards the end of the nineteenth century and reached its height in New Orleans round about 1917. Jazz was not wholly an African import, however, for added to the elements above were the sounds of the white military bands from Civil War days and Christian hymns imported from Europe, hymns which in turn had drawn on Italian nineteenth-century opera, English oratorio, and the German chorale. So the harmony and texture of jazz may reasonably be said to have been European in origin, and jazz itself is therefore a kind of synthesis; it was no longer what the slaves had sung in their native land, but the product of their response to their new environment, in rural slavery and urban exile. It was essentially the music of displaced, uprooted people, and subtle musical technicalities aside, it is perhaps that quality that most appealed to the composers who were attracted to it – Gershwin, Stravinsky, Milhaud, Hindemith, Villa-Lobos.

One profound difference between classical music and jazz is that jazz is essentially the music of the here and now. It is not interested in the past or the future; indeed its very origins lay in the need of the moment, to lift the slaves out of their predicament. Just as primitive music induces a state of trance or orgiastic enthusiasm, so jazz may lift us out of time. This has not prevented a great deal of jazz from becoming 'classic' in its own context, and the roll-call of great jazz musicians is a long and impressive one. It encompasses such legendary figures as Sidney Bechet, Jelly Roll Morton, Louis Armstrong – and a host of other Chicago stars in the Twenties – Fats Waller, Errol Garner, Duke Ellington, Dizzy Gillespie, Stan Getz and Miles Davis. That these names are all essentially those of performers only serves to emphasize the fact that jazz depends entirely on the here and now, quite unlike classical music, which has always existed in its own right, independent of individual performers.

This is not to deny that jazz has made an appreciable contribution to classical music in the sphere of rhythm, tonality and harmony, and

LEFT Aaron Copland (b. 1900), talking to Darius Milhaud (1892–1974).

ABOVE Copland conducting his work *El Salón Mexico* (1936) for BBC television in 1965.

particularly in the realm of instrumental colour. Would the clarinet, for example, not have been a poorer instrument if Gershwin had not used it so brilliantly in the opening of *Rhapsody in Blue*? One could also argue that jazz has, oddly enough, helped more people to hear – in the fullest sense – and appreciate polyphony, because it accustoms the listener to assimilating the effect of several independent voices or instruments playing simultaneously. Also, jazz has stimulated the process of free improvisation, which lifts the instrumentalist or singer from being simply a performer of written notes to being an all-round musician. However, the divide between jazz and serious or classical music has only been bridged in very superficial ways, precisely because of these essential differences. Benny Goodman playing Mozart remains inevitably a talented performer interpreting Mozart's music, which will survive as long as there are people to play it. Benny Goodman playing Benny Goodman, however, can only happen once. Or, to look at it another way, Stravinsky might write his *Ebony Concerto* for Woody Herman and his Boys, but the music remains for subsequent generations, long after Woody Herman has been forgotten.

So the conclusion must be that the two sorts of music will continue to exist side by side, with occasional glances in each other's direction, but nothing more; indeed it is perhaps desirable, and more healthy for both, that this should be so, for diversity has generally stimulated further development. Synthesis or convergence has nearly always tended to be symptomatic of the death of a tradition.

RIGHT Zoltán Kodály
(1882–1967).

ABOVE George Gershwin
(1898–1937),
photographed in London
in the 1930s.

Before leaving the Americas, reference must be made to Heitor Villa-Lobos (1887–1959) of Brazil, Carlos Chávez (b.1899) of Mexico, and Alberto Ginastera (b.1916) of Argentina. As one might expect from Latin Americans, their music has a decidedly nationalistic flavour enhanced by the richness of the cultural tradition. We now see a second wave of nationalism in the twentieth century. This time, however, it is a more mature, perhaps more impressive force to be reckoned with, and to take stock of it we must return to Europe, and to Hungary in particular.

Eastern Europe and folk music

Two composers are especially important for the work they did in the field of folk music – Zoltán Kodály (1882–1967) and Béla Bartók (1881–1945) – but whereas Kodály remained principally a national composer, Bartók was a figure of international importance. The whole approach to the collection of folk tunes had by their time become much more scientific. It was no longer a question of trying to transcribe them to fit into already formed melodic and harmonic moulds, but of discovering precisely what it was that gave them their individuality. Such analysis brought an awareness that the vast repertoire of folk music could enrich art music in a way that had never previously been realized. Bartók did not confine himself to Hungary and Romania in his search for folk music, but covered much of central Europe, and even visited Turkey and North Africa. In all he

ABOVE London's Royal
Festival Hall, built as part
of the 1951 Festival of
Britain, heralding the
country's postwar
recovery, and now, in an
enlarged form, the senior
member of the South
Bank complex; it has
rapidly established itself
as one of the world's
major concert halls.

RIGHT Perhaps no single
popular performer has
enjoyed such a following
from admirers all over the
world – both during his
life and posthumously –
as Elvis Presley, known to
many simply as 'The
King'.

published nearly two thousand tunes and wrote many books and articles about them. He also incorporated them into his music in a more profound way than had ever been done before, creating a genuine fusion between folk music and art music, rather than treating the folk element, as had so often happened in the past, simply as a decoration.

Had Bartók only achieved this he would have been an important figure in the history of music, but he was also a virtuoso pianist in his own right, and taught the piano at the Budapest Academy from 1907 to 1934. The fruits of this side of his career were the 153 piano pieces (1926–37) known as *Mikrokosmos*, published in six books. Apart from being of value in tuition, the books sum up Bartók's own piano

Sidney Bechet, saxophonist and clarinettist, was discovered at the age of eight, and played with several orchestras as a teenager in his birthplace, New Orleans. In 1918 he went to Chicago, and from there was launched on an international career, making his London debut a year later.

Miles Davis has been described as one of the 'poised and polished' exponents of the cool jazz that emerged after the Second World War, in contrast to the more extreme tonal effects of Stan Kenton and the music of slightly earlier performers such as Charlie Parker and Dizzy Gillespie.

LEFT The quartet of the Beatles was the greatest musical phenomenon of the 1960s, and for many they represent the highest achievement both of a pop group as a musical unit and of a native tradition of popular music-making in Britain.

ABOVE In the post-Beatles era groups proliferated and several styles succeeded one another, but in some cases lasting identities were established: seen here are The Clash.

technique and indicate many of the developments that took place in music in Europe in the first part of the twentieth century. It is perhaps not surprising that his own compositions, by common consent, will probably survive for posterity, along with those of a very few others from the first half of this century. Perhaps his quartets will prove to be his most significant contribution to form, and certainly one of the most significant to the medium, since Beethoven. He tended to use the piano more as a percussive instrument, which subsequent composers without his ear for sonorities have not done with the same skill, for he was a master of imagination when it came to conjuring new sonorities not only from the piano but also from percussion.

Bartók was above all a synthesizer. He summed up what had gone before rather than opening up a way for the future. For example, he did not suppress tonality – the key in which a work is written – but at times he used polytonality, or several keys at once. As a result the key centre is often hard to determine, and for the average listener polytonality often sounds the same as atonality, in which there is no key centre at all. He often used tone rows (that is, isolated successions of notes from which the music develops), or all the notes of the chromatic scale, and if he ever in fact evolved a technique based on this, he did not apply it with any consistency. Plainly, however, he is not only a nationalist, for the appeal of his music reaches beyond its purely national context. To a certain extent he exists in isolation, for he has had no direct successors and he founded no school. His situation expresses to a large extent the dilemma of Western music in the twentieth century. The course of musical history has taken some sharp turns in the past, but it seems as if the way ahead presents infinitely more problems, for there is no clear path to follow. Of course it may be argued that earlier composers did not always have a clear way ahead either. The difference is that they were never in the position of making a complete break with the past, or even of consciously choosing a path of development at all. Today a great number of alternatives present themselves, and therein lies the dilemma. As to how this situation arose we must go back to the full tide of German Romantic music once more, and see how it carried in it the seeds of its own destruction.

ABOVE Arnold Schönberg (1874–1951), photographed in Berlin in the 1930s, before he left Germany for France and, ultimately, America.

Schönberg and the development of atonality

The early music of Arnold Schönberg (1874–1951) is very much in the tradition of post-Romantic German music. His *Verklärte Nacht* (1899) is a string sextet that reflected Wagner in its chromaticism, while *Pelléas und Mélisande* (1903) is a symphonic poem in the tradition of Strauss. *Gurrelieder* (orchestrated in 1911) is a cantata that exceeds anything envisaged by Strauss or Mahler in terms of its sheer size, or by Wagner in its intensity of expression. But from about 1905 Schönberg was turning away from such monumental works

RIGHT Béla Bartók (1881–1945).

(although *Gurrelieder* was only completed with orchestration in 1911, it had to all intents and purposes been finished some ten years previously). In his later work Schönberg compressed or concentrated his musical language much more, and either went in for small groups of instruments, or, when still using the orchestra, preferred varied textures to huge washes of sound. He also carried to its logical conclusion the development implicit in Wagner's treatment of modulation, or moving from one key to another – the abandoning of tonality as it had been known, thereby arriving at atonality.

However, Schönberg rejected the term atonality, since it implies, strictly speaking, not having any tonality at all, and he much preferred the term pantonality, meaning including or embracing all the tonalities. This is evidently a much more positive interpretation of the concept, for it implies that rather than confining the music to any given centre of tonality, as was traditional, the composer has total freedom to move wherever he likes across the whole musical spectrum. Unfortunately the negative term, atonality, has now become the accepted one, so it is the one that we must use. It was one thing to see the tendencies that foreshadowed this development appearing incidentally or intermittently, as in certain passages of Wagner, but it was quite another to extract the concept and turn it into a formulated system.

What that system was, as formulated by Schönberg in 1923, became apparent after a period of six years' study and research, during which he composed no music. It was a method of composition using twelve tones related only to each other, in other words no longer related to a common centre, and was given the name dodecaphony, from the Greek, meaning twelve sounds. It was taken up by Schönberg's two chief followers, Alban Berg (1885–1935) and Anton von Webern (1883–1945), who both predeceased him. Berg was a much more lyrical composer, and seems to have related his music and his master's teaching to the past rather than taking it into the future. It is interesting, for example, that though Berg's opera *Wozzeck* (1917–21) is quite frequently produced, Schönberg's *Moses und Aaron* (1931–2, incomplete) has received less attention. Webern, on the other hand, went for a clear, open texture, but at the same time the strict economy of means and extreme concentration of the music make his compositions difficult for many people, and his output was in any case not prolific. Nevertheless one can see that, with such a momentous development, the unity of the musical world in the West has been broken, possibly for ever, and that future historians may well look upon the twentieth century in relation to the previous five centuries as we see the fourteenth century in relation to everything before it. Nor was the situation helped by those who jumped on the band-wagon of atonality and dodecaphony, and hailed it as the only way ahead, since those who were suspicious of it, or who reasonably doubted its ability to provide a future were driven on to the defensive, and therefore branded as reactionaries.

Anton von Webern (1883–1945), photographed *c.* 1935.

Neo-Classicism

In theory, at least, the musical forces in the first part of the twentieth century were ranged on totally opposite sides of the divide, since the most clearly discernible tendency that did not conform with Schönberg was neo-Classicism. It can be seen in Russia, in the music of Sergei Prokofiev (1891–1953), to some extent in that of Dmitri Shostakovich (1906–75), and of course in the work of Igor Stravinsky, to whom we shall return; to some degree all three may also be regarded as another generation of nationalist composers. In France it was taken up by Arthur Honneger (1892–1955), who was of Swiss origin, Darius Milhaud (1892–1974), and Francis Poulenc (1899–1963). It is also evident in the music of the Englishman Benjamin Britten (1913–76), the American Aaron Copland, and the German Paul Hindemith (1895–1963).

The unifying aspect of all these composers was their ability to speak in a musical language that people could still understand. All were concerned at the changes that had taken place, and determined to provide music that would be part of people's lives, not an increasingly rarefied indulgence or an ordeal to be avoided. Communication and craftsmanship were therefore key elements in their music, as was tonality, though that did not prevent them from using tone rows, for example.

This was not necessarily a view with which Stravinsky would have identified, however, and some aspects of it would have been totally unacceptable to him. He burst upon the world in 1913 with his ballet *The Rite of Spring*, surely the apotheosis of primitivism, but ten years later had abandoned that concept for neo-Classicism, which remained his predominant style until 1951. His opera *The Rake's Progress* marked another turning point in his career, and in his later works he adopted the techniques of Schönberg and Webern, thus throwing into confusion such ardent admirers as Nadia Boulanger, who had resolutely set her face against atonality. It said a great deal for her musicianship and her ability as a teacher that eventually she was able to make the adjustment, though probably no one other than Stravinsky would have been able to induce her to contemplate it. The assimilation by Stravinsky of Schönberg's technique was in any case gradual and selective, and was no overnight, miraculous conversion.

It is difficult with a composer like Stravinsky to assess all the different elements in his long career while at the same time pointing out its essential unity. One cannot dismiss a composer of his stature and influence as simply eclectic. He was too fine a musician, for one thing. He ought more properly to be seen first as a consummate artist, especially in the field of rhythm, harmony and orchestration, and then as a catalyst of the music of the early and mid-twentieth century. He helped to sum up the Western musical tradition rather than attempting to show the path ahead. Certainly from his own writings he saw his function as a composer as essentially one of creativity through the traditional means of accepted limits. As he wrote in

RIGHT Benjamin Britten and Yehudi Menuhin rehearsing Mozart's violin sonata in A major, K.401, in 1955 at the Red House, Britten's home at Aldeburgh, Suffolk. In July 1945 they had made a tour together of German concentration camps, giving violin and piano recitals.

LEFT Benjamin Britten photographed in October 1949 with the novelist E. M. Forster, who wrote the libretto for Britten's opera *Billy Budd*, and was always a devoted friend.

Poetics of Music: 'Whatever diminishes constraint diminishes strength. The more constraint one imposes, the more one frees oneself of the chains that shackle the spirit.'

The immediate musical past

In the third quarter of the twentieth century Stravinsky's doctrine has not been a particularly fashionable one. So-called liberalizing tendencies have had the concomitant effect of undervaluing formal education, and people have been encouraged simply to express themselves, irrespective of whether they have anything at all to express. Indeed the very concept of 'liberal' has almost come to be identified with nihilism; critical and moral faculties are blurred, and responsibilities are abrogated. In the realm of music the composer is in an unenviable position, since he will be condemned either as too avant-garde or too traditional, according to taste. It is only in the realm of the performance of music, where formal education is still necessary, that standards continue to improve, and we are blessed with a seemingly endless succession of gifted artists. Indeed, if it were not so, some contemporary composers would never have their works performed.

However, before turning to contemporary music, one composer remains to be considered, since he defies classification and yet is a highly important present-day figure, not only for his own compositions, but also for the composers he has taught. Olivier Messiaen (b.1908) may be regarded as a product of the French musical tradition, since he studied with Dukas at the Paris Conservatoire and taught there himself, and was also one of the succession of great French organists. He studied with Dupré, and is still organist of the church of the Trinité in Paris. Like Stravinsky, he was extremely eclectic in the elements he assimilated (birdsong, for example), and those elements which he does employ are hard to distinguish in his intensely personal music. What is perhaps even more remarkable is that he has taught so many celebrated pupils, but has founded no school or genre of music; each pupil has developed in his own way. They include such different musical personalities as Pierre Boulez (b.1925), Karlheinz Stockhausen (b.1928), Luigi Nono (b.1924) and Iannis Xenakis (b.1922). Messiaen forms an important link between the composers of the first half of the twentieth century and those of the second.

Igor Stravinsky
(1882–1971).

The cover for Stravinsky's *Ragtime* (1918), designed by Picasso. In this work Stravinsky was making a deliberate attempt to re-create the spirit of early American jazz.

Where exactly one puts the century's turning-point is somewhat arbitrary, though the year most frequently used is 1945, the end of the Second World War, a convenient date because it is almost mid-century, and because the war was a phenomenon of such magnitude. There was a period of artistic stagnation for some long time after the war, until the dislocation it caused was overcome. Thus although the performance of Benjamin Britten's opera *Peter Grimes* in London in 1945 seems to coincide with a new post-war era, it in fact marked the completion of work that he had begun long before. Romanticism had been a long time dying, and when it eventually did so, it was with Richard Strauss's sumptuous *Four Last Songs* of 1948. That year saw another work of great significance, Messiaen's *Turangalîla* symphony, and one is tempted therefore to take 1948, with its neatly dovetailed works that represent such divergent aesthetics, as the turning-point of the twentieth century. It was also the year that René Leibowitz (1913–72), the apostle of dodecaphony, went to Darmstadt for the international holiday courses for new music held there. Instituted in 1946, the courses had attracted Hindemith, who taught there in 1947, and Messiaen who went there in 1949, though after Leibowitz' visit Webern was adoped as the spiritual father of the Darmstadt group.

The present and the future

In charting the musical waters of one's own time one has to steer between the Scylla of attempting to forecast the future trends as represented by a select few, and the Charybdis of swamping the reader with a mass of names. Either way one is very likely soon to be

Olivier Messiaen (b. 1908) at the console of his organ at the Trinité church in Paris.

231

LEFT Pierre Boulez (b. 1925), as well as being a composer, is a distinguished conductor and a particularly sensitive interpreter of the works of Debussy.

BELOW LEFT Richard Strauss (1864–1949) and Sir Thomas Beecham during preparations for a concert in London's Drury Lane theatre in 1947.

ABOVE Sir Thomas Beecham (1879–1961) had no hesitation in re-orchestrating composers' works when he felt that he knew best, but he brought an enormous enthusiasm to music, and an ability to communicate that enthusiasm to players and audience. In particular he enjoyed French music.

proved wrong. Doubtless, future music historians will in retrospect see certain patterns emerging and similarities between composers who seem very different in their tendencies now. There will always be a Vivaldi somewhere, forgotten immediately after his lifetime – or even during it – only to be resurrected by subsequent generations and hailed as the creator of the concerto; even Stravinsky dismissed Vivaldi without realizing his importance.

Nevertheless there are certain historical lines that can be traced to the present day, and one of them is the Darmstadt *Ferienkurse* already referred to. Among its first developments was total serialization, an extension of the principles of tonal serialization as advanced by Schönberg. This meant that the basic tone row could be used backwards as well as forwards, and inverted too, in almost endless variations. If the tones could be serialized, then so could all the other elements of music, such as timbre, dynamics, duration, silences. Boulez took this up, but his innate musicality has made a work such as *Le marteau sans maître* (1954, revised 1957) more rewarding than might otherwise seem likely from such a system as total serialization.

Lennox Berkeley (b. 1903) and Yehudi Menuhin discussing a performance of the composer's Violin Concerto at a concert in Bath Abbey in 1961.

He had also been attracted to *musique concrète* in the early 1950s, as can be seen from his *Etudes* I and II, but that was obviously not to be the way forward for him, and he soon abandoned it.

Musique concrète involved transforming or distorting musical tones, or any other naturally produced sounds, by electronic means and recording them on tape. Its essential feature was that the sounds were in origin natural, but as composers became aware of the wide variety of sounds that might be generated by electronic means in the studio, they saw this as a new field of experiment. There was an intermediate stage when natural sounds were mixed with electronic ones, as, for example, in Stockhausen's *Gesang der Jünglinge* (1956) and a few subsequent works, and from there to total electronic sound was a short and logical step.

Stockhausen had also encountered *musique concrète*, but preferred working with pure electronic music in the early 1950s, as we have seen; at the same time, however, he published serial works such as *Kreuzspiel* (1952), the first four *Klavierstücke* (1953) and *Kontra Punkte* (the same year). Since then he has experimented in several

John Cage (b. 1912) with David Tudor at the Royal Albert Hall in London in May 1972.

directions, though the works of the early 1970s have tended to be more conservative. Stockhausen has a large following from almost every country of the world with any pretensions to musical culture, and yet his music remains for the most part – at least for the time being – beyond the reach of the average music-lover. Communication is not the prime concern of his music, nor is expression or expressiveness high on his list of priorities.

Serialization had made headway in America, meanwhile, in the works of Milton Babbit (b.1916). A very early admirer of Charles Ives, Henry Cowell (1897–1965) had experimented with piano tone clusters, and his pupil John Cage (b.1912) developed the prepared piano in which the timbre and pitch were altered by attaching objects to the strings. Earle Brown (b.1926) has experimented with aleatoric music, in which the element of chance – somewhat paradoxically – plays a determining role. Elliott Carter (b.1908), who had been a rather cautious modernist until then, began experimenting in the late 1940s with metrical modulation, which was basically an asymmetrical system of changing speed. Edgar Varèse (1883–1965), a Parisian who emigrated to America, more or less embarked on a new career when he took up electronic music in the 1950s.

The trans-Atlantic cross-fertilization is stronger now than ever before, and Cage and Stockhausen influence composers around the world. Certain Europeans, such as the Hungarian György Ligeti (b.1923), the Poles Witold Lutoslawski (b.1913) and Krzysztof Penderecki (b.1933), and the Italians Luigi Dallapiccola (b.1904), his pupil Luciano Berio (b.1923), and Luigi Nono (who married Schönberg's daughter Nuria) may well be better known in the future than in their own lifetimes. But here one is falling into the clutches of both Scylla and Charybdis simultaneously, and hovering in the background are those words of Schönberg: 'Contemporaries are not final judges, but are generally overruled by history.' Beethoven, after all, had to take comfort from much the same words.

An additional dilemma – and a very real one – for the professional musician today just as much as for the music-lover is the very abundance of music available, on radio and television, on record players and cassettes, even forced upon us from muzak and peripatetic transistors. We are engulfed in sound, to the extent that our capacity for absorbing it suffers. At the same time, we have much greater possibilities for manipulating what we hear. Confronted with this situation, it is perhaps not surprising that the music-lover takes refuge in what he knows and likes, and to a large degree the composer pursues his way in isolation.

Here the responsible critic can play an important role in bringing to public attention works that he considers especially noteworthy, and enlightened patronage – which still exists – can help in arranging performances of new music. And we must be prepared for some works that are less than satisfactory. Our modern obsession with comparative ratings will not ensure that we always get the best. In any

OVERLEAF Karlheinz Stockhausen (b. 1928) conducting his *Inori* at the Coliseum Theatre in London in October 1974.

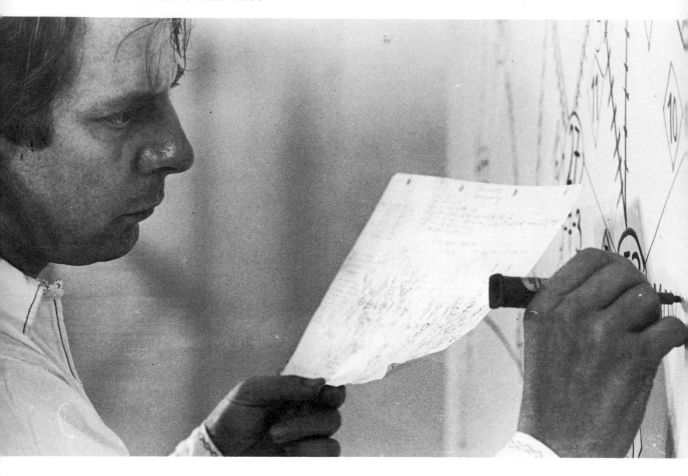

Stockhausen preparing his graph of the Mantra.

case, our critical faculties would benefit from some healthy exercise; otherwise they may atrophy. We must work together to restore the global conception of music. As far as performers are concerned, some regard contemporary music as a challenge, and some have even made it a cause; many more are obliged to accept it in order to live. There is no need for people to choose between the accepted and the avant-garde; a more tolerant attitude towards both would work wonders. For any performance one needs a trinity of composer, performer and public, and they must all be willing to listen open-mindedly if music is to have a future.

In an age when technology has become a part of everyone's daily life, we must be prepared for the fact that there may well be a totally new world of sonorities to discover. At the same time, those who are trying to explore and interpret that world must have more patience with, and respect for, the works of the past, if only because without them they would not be able to understand their art today. Ultimately, however, if music ceases to have a human dimension, it may no longer validly claim identity with the main stream of Western music, for its fundamental concern has always been humanity, even

238

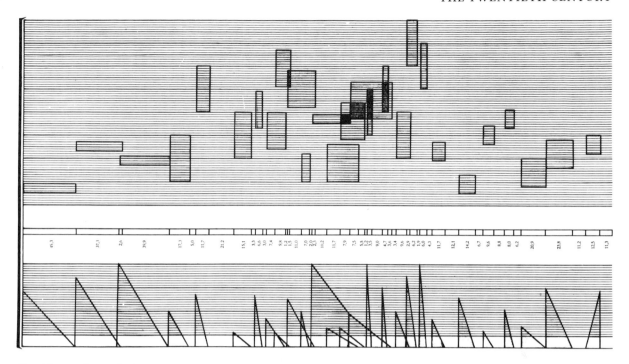

Stockhausen's musical notation bears little resemblance to conventional scores, since he makes frequent use of electronic devices, requiring special training for performers and technicians alike.

RIGHT The Ondes Martenot, named after its inventor, Maurice Martenot, and first exhibited in 1928; it is one of the few electrical instruments to have been accepted by the majority of composers, doubtless because it is melodic.

From here until p.34 players must try to interpret on their instrument the pictures assigned to them.
Each picture interpretation should last about 20 seconds, but the conductor may extend or shorten
this depending on how he feels the interpretation is going. Go from one picture to the next without a break.

The demands made by composers on performers now extend to the interpretation of pictures in place of a conventional musical score, as in David Bedford's *With 100 Kazoos.*

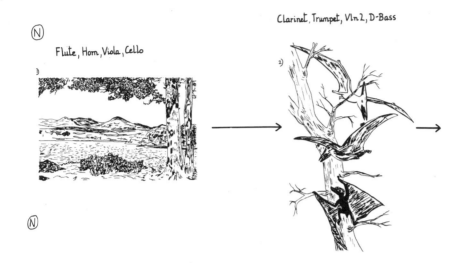

Flute, Horn, Viola, Cello

Clarinet, Trumpet, Vln 2, D-Bass

when composers like Beethoven have had to accept that they were ahead of their time, and resign themselves to leaving many in their audience behind. The danger of our losing the human dimension is far greater today than it has ever been ; it seems as likely to happen in the realm of pop music as at the opposite end of the spectrum, and the whole is vitiated by commercialism. Popular music as opposed to art music was, until comparatively recently, the everyday music of society. It embraced what was left of the folk tradition, the songs of the music halls and the drawing-room ballads, and included a strong element of dance band music, which was given a powerful boost with the arrival of jazz. The inter-war years – the 1920s and 1930s – saw an amazing expansion of this music: musicals and reviews flourished, there was a frenzy of dances and parties, and apparently music everywhere. Since gramophones and the radio allowed popular music to reach a much wider audience than ever before, new tunes, dances, bands and singers became famous very quickly. In many of the popular tunes and rhythms there was a large degree of sophistication and of unity, so that from hot jazz to the romantic ballad was a continuous spectrum, and, most important of all, people experienced it at first hand, and were directly involved in it.

The advent of talking pictures was perhaps the most significant stage in the removal of the truly popular element from music. This new medium rapidly became highly professional, but in so doing it diverted traditional sources of talent and popular music-making into a great new industry, where taste was dictated to the millions by a very few. This is not to imply that the cinema did not inspire some fine artistic creations. From the point of view of individual

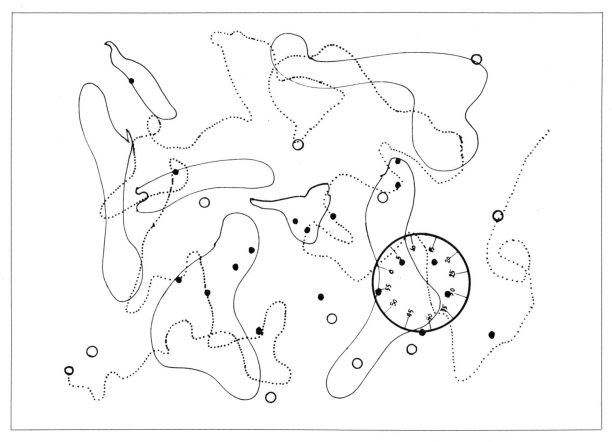

John Cage's *Cartridge Music*, sheet number seven.

involvement in the making and enjoyment of popular music, however, a vital element had been destroyed. People no longer participated directly; they had become onlookers, encouraged to emulate as best they could what was meant to be their music, their way of life. Of course one could claim that the same trend towards depersonalization of music-making also occurred in the sphere of classical music, but it is true to say that people who listen to serious music tend on the whole to go to concerts and operas, and are therefore more aware of the concept of the live performance; indeed, most of them only accept recordings as a substitute for a live performance.

The onset of the Second World War to a large extent camouflaged this depersonalization, since the dislocation of normal life was made more bearable when there was a continuous supply of music and light entertainment, from the radio primarily but also in dance halls, cinemas and theatres. In the immediate postwar years the cinema again asserted its hold, promoting stars such as Bing Crosby and Frank Sinatra who were already established, and producing new ones such as Elvis Presley. Times were changing, however, and there were two major new developments. The first was the impact of television, which broke the monopoly of the cinema industry, and certainly

OVERLEAF Glen Miller's orchestra, as it appeared in the film *Sun Valley Serenade*. The pianist is the actor John Payne.

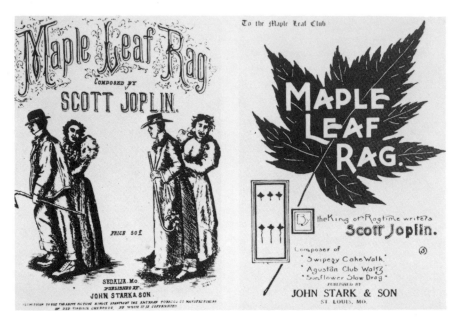

LEFT An early edition of *Maple Leaf Rag* by Scott Joplin (1868–1917), prolific American composer and pianist, mainly of ragtime, whose music was re-discovered and enormously popularized by cinema and ballet in the 1970s.

BELOW Django Reinhardt (second from right) with the Quintet of the Hot Club of France, which included the violinist Stephane Grapelli (far left), photographed in the 1930s.

destroyed its role as the sole creator of mass culture. The second development was a revolt against the somewhat exhausted traditional romantic ballad of the 'roses in June' variety, or the harmless 'nonsense' song with its easily memorized words and tune. It is interesting from both a sociological and musical viewpoint that the revolt should have produced the pop group, represented supremely by the Beatles.

For virtually the first time since the development of mass media, and possibly even earlier, a musical tradition emerged with roots in the life of society. That society was mirrored with devastating accuracy in the lyrics of songs such as 'Eleanor Rigby', 'She's leaving home' or 'When I'm sixty-four', songs about parking meters, paperbacks and LSD. Above all, from the musical angle, there was a fresh stream of melody and harmonic sense that seemed to catch the mood of the times and give expression to much that had been latent in the popular postwar musical subconscious. Of course much of the music of the Beatles was a distillation of what had gone before, but in a haunting tune such as 'Yesterday' they articulated a sentiment that captured more than the mood of the time.

Needless to say, all of this rapidly became big business. Groups proliferated, and, in the constant search for new talent, artificial stimulus was given to pop music on a vast scale. Without that stimulus many performers and tendencies would never have been noticed. The mass media played a considerable part in this development, which had nothing to do with music as such. Moreover, an obsession with the more outrageous aspects of the world of pop music has tended to eclipse some of the more positive aspects of the phenomenon, such as the fact that people have been encouraged to make much more music of their own, and even if some of them have little talent, at least they are actively participating once more. The less spectacular nature of folk music and its executants means that it receives less exposure, but it gives pleasure to a great many and again involves people in live music-making, though the music itself no longer has much claim to being folk music as it has been known in the past.

Pop music draws on the highly sophisticated techniques available in the recording studio, and in a way continues the relationship that existed in the past between composer and instrument-maker. The one acts as a stimulus to the other in evolving new techniques and compositions. Pop music now plays an immense part in many people's lives. In an increasingly stressful environment it can be an important aid to relaxation, though it has the dubious concomitant effect of heightening the general noise level, as some performers have discovered to their cost. In an increasingly impersonal world, pop music brings a dimension that many people evidently feel is lacking in their lives. One may accept the commercialism, since it is equally present, if less obviously so, in the sphere of classical music, but if pop music ceases to be a celebration of life, and becomes a substitute

LEFT Bob Dylan has made a lasting impression on the field of popular music through the individuality of his style and the serious content of his songs.

for it, that would be a matter for great regret. Hopefully pop music can take care of itself, and in time a talent similar to that of the Beatles will emerge somewhere.

The problem is not so very different in the world of classical music, or 'legit' as it is sometimes deferentially known in the pop world. The search for a way ahead is unceasing, and it is only less frenetic in its search than the pop world because it has minority appeal and far fewer people are engaged in it. Often the end product seems little different in its lack of the human dimension. But there is no ready solution; the composer has only his integrity to rely on, and that can be the only possible way forward for us all.

RIGHT The BBC Radiophonic Workshop in 1974, which boasts a large-voltaged controlled electronic music synthesizer with digital memory, eight-track tape machine and reduction mixer.

List of Key Works

*c.*1304–1377 MACHAUT, Guillaume de
Messe de Notre Dame
Je puis trop bien (*ballade*)

*c.*1450–1521 JOSQUIN DES PRES
Adieu mes Amours (*chanson*)
Missa Pange Lingua

1567–1643 MONTEVERDI, Claudio
Vespers of 1610
Hor ch'el Ciel e la Terra (*madrigal*)
[La Favola d'] Orfeo (*opera*)

1678–1741 VIVALDI, Antonio
12 concerti, Opus 8 (Trial of
Harmony and Invention), in
particular nos. 1, 2, 3 and 4: 'The
Four Seasons'

1685–1750 BACH, Johann Sebastian
No. 2 in F from Brandenburg
Concerti, BWV 1046–51
The Well-Tempered Clavier,
BWV 846–893 (*48 preludes and
fugues*)
Toccata and Fugue in D minor for
organ, BWV 565
St Matthew Passion, BWV 244
Wachet Auf, BWV 645 (*chorale
prelude*)
Suite no. 2 in B minor, BWV 1067

1685–1759 HANDEL, George
Water Music suite
Messiah (*oratorio*)
Zadok the Priest (*coronation anthem*)
Harpsichord suite no. 7

1732–1809 HAYDN, Josef
Symphony no. 94 in G ('Surprise')
Piano sonata no. 52 in E flat
String quartet, no. 2 in F, Opus 77
The Creation (*oratorio*)
Trumpet concerto in E flat

1756–1791 MOZART, Wolfgang
Symphony no. 41 in C, K551

('Jupiter')
Piano sonata no. 11 in A, K331
Clarinet quintet in A, K581
Serenade no. 13 in G for strings,
K525 (Eine Kleine Nachtmusik)
The Marriage of Figaro, K492 (*opera*)
Mass no. 19 in D minor, K626
(*requiem Mass*)

1770–1827 BEETHOVEN, Ludwig van
Symphony no. 5 in C minor, Opus 67
Symphony no. 6 in F, Opus 68
('Pastoral')
String quartet no. 16 in F, Opus 135
Piano sonata no. 8 in C minor, Opus
13 ('Pathétique')
Piano sonata no 23 in F minor, Opus
57 ('Appassionata')
Piano concerto no. 5 in E flat
('Emperor')
Mass in D, Opus 123 (Missa Solemnis)
Sonata for violin and piano no. 5 in
F, Opus 24 ('Spring')

1797–1828 SCHUBERT, Franz
Symphony no. 8 in B minor, D759
('Unfinished')
Impromptus nos. 1–8 for piano,
D899 & D935
Piano quintet in A, D667 ('The Trout')
Die Schöne Mullerin, D795 (*song cycle*)

1803–1869 BERLIOZ, Hector
Symphonie Fantastique, Opus 14

1809–1847 MENDELSSOHN, Felix
Songs without Words (*piano*)
Concerto for violin and orchestra in
E minor, Opus 64
Hebrides overture, Opus 26
('Fingal's Cave')

1810–1849 CHOPIN, Frederic
Etude no. 12, Opus 10
Prelude no. 15, Opus 28

Concerto for piano and orchestra no.
1 in E minor, Opus 11

1810–1856 SCHUMANN, Robert
Kinderscenen, Opus 15 (*piano*)
Dichterliebe, Opus 48 (*song cycle*)
Piano quintet in E flat, Opus 44

1813–1883 WAGNER, Richard
Die Walküre, Part 2 of Der Ring des
Nibelungen (*opera*)
Overture to The Flying Dutchman

1813–1901 VERDI, Giuseppe
La Traviata (*opera*)
Requiem Mass

1824–1896 BRUCKNER, Anton
Symphony no. 4 in E flat
('Romantic')
Mass no. 2 in E minor

1825–1899 STRAUSS, Johann
The Blue Danube waltz, Opus 314
Die Fledermaus (*operetta*)

1833–1897 BRAHMS, Johannes
Symphony no. 2 in D, Opus 73
Rhapsody for alto, chorus and
orchestra, Opus 53
German Requiem, Opus 45
Clarinet quintet in B minor, Opus 115

1840–1893 TCHAIKOVSKY, Peter
Piano concerto no. 1 in B flat minor,
Opus 23
1812 Overture, Opus 49
The Nutcracker suite, Opus 71a

1841–1904 DVORAK, Antonin
Symphony no. 9 in E minor, Opus 95
('From the New World')
Slavonic Dances no. 3 in A flat, Opus
46, no. 10 in E minor, Opus 72
Concerto for cello and orchestra in B
minor, Opus 104

1857–1934 ELGAR, Edward
Variations on an original theme,
Opus 36 ('Enigma')
Concerto for cello and orchestra in E
minor, Opus 85

1860–1911 MAHLER, Gustav
Symphony no. 1 in D
Songs of a Travelling Wayfarer

1862–1918 DEBUSSY, Claude
Prélude à l'après-midi d'un faune
Suite Bergamasque, including no. 3
'Clair de Lune'
La Mer

1864–1949 STRAUSS, Richard
Also sprach Zarathrustra, Opus 30

1865–1957 SIBELIUS, Jean
Finlandia, Opus 26
Concerto for violin and orchestra in
D minor, Opus 47

1874–1951 SCHOENBERG, Arnold
Pierrot Lunaire, Opus 21 (*song cycle*)

1881–1945 BARTOK, Béla
Mikrokosmos (*piano*)
Music for Strings, Percussion and
Celeste

1882–1971 STRAVINSKY, Igor
The Rite of Spring (*ballet*)
The Firebird (*ballet*)

1898–1937 GERSHWIN, George
Rhapsody in Blue

b.1908 MESSIAEN, Olivier
Turangalila symphony
Transports de Joie, from
'L'Ascension'

1913–1976 BRITTEN, Benjamin
Peter Grimes, Opus 33 (*opera*)
Winter Words, Opus 52 (*song cycle*)

b.1928 STOCKHAUSEN, Karlheinz
Kontakte

b.1933 PENDERECKI, Krysztof
Threnedy for the Victims of
Hiroshima

Glossary

Acoustics In general the science of hearing, and in music the way in which sound is transmitted to the ear.

Antiphonal Relating to the practice of singing and playing alternately, where two choirs or groups of instruments perform in different parts of a church or concert platform.

Aria An air or song, usually extended, in an opera or oratorio.

Arioso A vocal movement halfway between recitative (*q.v.*) and aria. It is of a declamatory nature, but is sung in strict time.

Bar Originally a vertical line between musical notes (now called the barline) which was placed at irregular intervals and served as an aid to the eye. Barlines now correspond to the metrical accent of the music and are placed at regular intervals, while 'bar' refers to the interval between them.

Cantata A sacred or secular composition of a dramatic nature, though not for stage performance, consisting of aria and recitative (*qq.v.*). It may be for solo voice and continuo (*q.v.*), or solo, chorus and several instruments.

Cantor Choir director in a cathedral or collegiate church.

Cantus firmus Originally a section of plainsong used as a melodic base on which the rest of a composition might be constructed; subsequently secular material was also employed.

Carol A song with a refrain, at first associated with dance, later with seasons of the Church's year, and, more recently, with Christmas.

Chorale Generally a hymn melody of the German Lutheran Church, to be sung by the congregation.

Chord A combination of notes sounded simultaneously.

Chromaticism, chromatic scale The chromatic scale, now the basis of Western music, is made up of twelve successive semitones or halftones. A melody or harmony that uses these notes or an instrument that is able to produce them is said to be chromatic, and chromaticism is the use of these tones when they do not occur in the usual scale (see *Key*).

Coloratura Elaborate vocal music that is 'coloured' or figured with ornaments and runs.

Concerted music Music for voices or instruments that is arranged in parts.

Concerto, concerto grosso A concerto is usually an extended composition for solo instrument accompanied by orchestra, whereas *concerto grosso* is for a group of instruments accompanied by orchestra. In both the essential feature is the element of contrast.

Concord A chord (*q.v.*) that sounds pleasing or satisfying in itself. Since this is a very subjective criterion, the definition of concord has altered considerably as music has developed.

Continuo A part played continuously during a composition, usually consisting of a bass stringed instrument and lute or keyboard instrument, hence *basso continuo* or, in English, thorough or through bass.

Counterpoint, contrapuntal Music that consists mainly of two or more simultaneous lines of melody, sometimes with additional material.

Counter-tenor A male alto voice similar in range to a high tenor or female contralto.

Dodecaphony (from the Greek meaning 'twelve tones') Music in which the tones of the chromatic scale are used systematically in a certain order, or derivations of that order, throughout a composition.

Dynamics Variation in volume.

Fantasia Usually an instrumental composition of no fixed form.

Fugue A word originally applied to a canon, where the melodic subject was repeated exactly by a voice or voices, and later to a type or style of contrapuntal (*q.v.*) composition where the melodic subject was developed in imitation.

Impresario Organizer or manager of operatic or orchestral company.

Kapellmeister Conductor of an opera, orchestra or choir.

Key The melodic and harmonic identity of a piece of music is established by a succession of eight notes, known as a scale, starting from any one of the twelve notes of the chromatic scale (*q.v.*). The starting note is known as the keynote or tonic, and the fifth note is the dominant.

Leitmotif A recurring theme that is always associated with a particular person, sentiment or situation – particularly to be found in Wagner's operas.

Libretto The words or text of an opera or oratorio, written by the librettist and set to music by the composer.

Monophony A single, unaccompanied line of melody, as opposed to polyphony (*q.v.*).

Obbligato A vocal or instrumental part that is an essential feature of a composition.

Oratorio A poem or sacred text set to music on a large scale, with soloists, chorus and instruments. A Passion is an oratorio on the

subject of the Crucifixion, though the earliest ones were unaccompanied.

Polyphony (from the Greek meaning 'many voices') Music with two or more lines of melody (see *counterpoint*), as opposed to monophony (*q.v.*).

Prima donna The leading soprano ('first lady') in an opera.

Recitative Vocal writing that follows the natural speech rhythms and inflections, with minimal instrumental accompaniment.

Rondo Basically a form in which the first subject is reintroduced, sometimes several times, after additional material has been played or sung.

Sequence A liturgical text sung between the Gradual and the Gospel on particular days, latterly much like a hymn. Also a reptition of a phrase at different points in the scale.

Sonata A composition for one instrument or two (e.g. piano and violin), normally in three or four movements contrasted in speed and rhythm but related in key. In sonata form, better termed first movement form, two successive themes are developed and repeated.

Swell-box Part of the pipework of an organ enclosed in a box with

shutters that may be opened and closed to increase or decrease volume.

Symphony A composition for full orchestra that developed from the Italian overture. Normally it consists of three or four contrasting movements though occasionally it is continuous.

Syncopation The moving of a normal accent either from a strong beat to a weak one or vice versa, so that the expected pattern is reversed, and a jazz-like effect is obtained.

Tempo Literally 'time', but more precisely the speed at which a piece of music is played.

Tonality The focal harmonic centre of a piece of music, usually identified by its key (*q.v.*). 'Atonality' means having no such key, 'polytonality' having several tonalities, and 'pantonality' embracing all tonalities.

Tone clusters A number of adjacent notes played simultaneously, a technique used in modern piano music, though similar effects can be obtained from other instruments.

Tone rows The notes used in twelve-tone composition (see *Dodecaphony*).

Virtuoso A performer especially skilled in instrumental or vocal technique.

Acknowledgments

Photographs were supplied or are reproduced by kind permission of the following. (Page numbers in italics indicate colour pictures; primary sources appear in roman type, secondary sources in italics.)

The picture on page 116 is reproduced by gracious permission of HM the Queen

Aberdeen Art Gallery: 157 (photo Studio Morgan)

Alinari, Florence, *Weidenfeld & Nicolson Archives*: 29, 44, 45, 54–5, 68–9, 74

Archaeological Museum, Delphi: 11

Archiv fur Kunst und Geschichte, Berlin: 53, 80 above, *99, 107, 147* above and below, *151, 154–5, 155* above *159,* 171 left and right, 172–3, 179 left, 186, 187, 196, 197 right, 198 above and below, 212 above and below right, *214, 215,* 224, 225, 226

Ashmolean Museum, Oxford: 84; *Weidenfeld & Nicholson Archives 103* bottom left

Associated Press, London: 232 below left

Erich Auerbach, London: 216 right, 220

Clive Barda, London: 232 above

Bayerisches Nationalmuseum, Munich: 50

Bayerische Staatsbibliothek, Munich: *102*

BBC Hulton Picture Library, London: 220–1, 217 left, 228

BBC Pictorial Publicity, London: 247

Biblioteca Ambrosiana, Milan: 15

Biblioteca Apostolica, Vaticana: 89 above

Biblioteca Communale, Palermo, *Weidenfeld & Nicolson Archives*: 183

Biblioteca del Conservatorio, Venice, *Alan Kendall Collection*: 91

Biblioteca Universitaria, Turin: 89

Bibliothek Etense, Modena, *Scala*: 98–9

Bibliothèque Nationale, Paris: 14, 26, 28, 30–1, 40, 63 below, 92 above, 93, 94–5, 202; *Hamlyn Group Picture Library 38; Weidenfeld and Nicolson Archives* 204

Biecz Museum, Poland: 104

Bildarchiv des Österreichische Nationalbibliothek, Vienna: 134, *Weidenfeld & Nicolson Archives* 136 below, 168–9, 176 left and right, 177

Bildarchiv Foto Marburg: 78, 115

Boosey & Hawkes Ltd., London: 230

British Library, London: 8, 17, 21, 23, 27, 36, 77, 112 below, 112, 130, 138 above and below, 139; *Weidenfeld & Nicolson Archives* 98

By kind permission of the Trustees of the British Museum, London, *Weidenfeld & Nicolson Archives*: 80, 90

Chateau de Versailles, *Hamlyn Group Picture Library : 155* below

J & W Chester/Wilhelm Hansen London Ltd: 231 left

Civica Raccolta Stampe Achille Bertarelli, Milan: 82–3

Civico Museo Bibliografico, Bologna: 87

Corcoran Gallery of Art, Washington DC: 112 above

Deutsches Museum, Munich: 108 above

Escorial Library, Spain, *MAS*: 22, 24–5, *38–9, 42* above and below

Faculty of Music, Oxford University: 62, 86

David Farrell, Gloucester: 233

Fondazione Giorio Cini Istituto de Storia dell'arte, Venice: 117 above

Gallerie Pinacoteca di Brera, Milan: 48

Gemeentemuseum, The Hague: 175; *Weidenfeld & Nicolson Archives* 121

Germanisches Nationalmuseum, Nuremburg: 108 below; *Hamlyn Group Picture Library* 57

Glasgow University Library: *39*

Gesellschaft der Musikfreunde, Vienna: 212 left

Giraudon, Paris: 145, *210–1*

Herzog Anton Ulrich Museum, Brunswick: 70

Historisches Museum der Stadt Wien, Vienna: 137, 161, 164

Horniman Museum, London: 74–5

Interfoto MTI, Budapest: 217 right

International Freelance Library, London: 229 (Kurt Hutton)

Internationale Stiftung Mozarteum, Salzburg, *Weidenfeld & Nicolson Archives*: 135

Alan Kendall Collection: 143, 149, 152

Kunsthistorisches Museum, Vienna/Gesellschaft der Musikfreunde, Vienna: 60; *Weidenfeld & Nicolson Archives 103* bottom right

Librarie Larousse, Paris, *Hamlyn Group Picture Library*: 239 below

Susie Maeder, London: *218*

Mander & Mitchenson Theatre Collection, London: 117 below

Mansell Collection, London: 71

MAS, Barcelona: *42* below

Memling Museum, St John's Hospital, Bruges: half-title page

Musée des Beaux Arts, Rouen, *Giraudon*: 20

Musée du Louvre, Paris: 10, 88 (Photo Musées Nationaux, Paris)

Musée Instrumental du Conservatoire National de Musique, Paris: 5

Musée Picardy, Amiens: 153

Museo Cirico, Turin: 140

Museo del Prado, Madrid: 36–7, 76

Museo Nazionale, Naples, *Scala : 35*

Museo Teatrale alla Scala, Milan: 96, 185; *Weidenfeld & Nicolson Archives 184*

Museum für Geschichte der Stadt, Leipzig: 114

Museum für Hamburgische Geschichte Bildarchiv, Hamburg: 87

Museum voor Schone Kunsten, Antwerp: *Scala 46, 47*

Musikinstrumenten-Museum der Karl-Marx-Universitat, Leipzig, *Weidenfeld & Nicolson Archives*: 69

Narodni Museum, Prague: 141

National Gallery, London: *43, 106, 111, 150*

National Museum, Copenhagen, *Hamlyn Group Picture Library*: 21

National Portrait Gallery, London: *107* left, 208–9, 213

Newberry Library, Chicago: 64–5

C.F.Peters Corporation, New York: 241

Photo Mali, Charenton: 231 right

David Redfern, London: *219* (photo Stephen Morley), *222* (photo Ray Green), *223* (photo Stephen Morley)

Report, London: 234 (photo Chris Davies), 236–7, 238 (photos Peter Harrap)

Richard-Wagner-Gedenkstratte, Bayreuth: 118–9

Robert-Schumann-Haus, Zwickau: 170

Royal College of Music, London: 92 below (Windsor Collection); *Weidenfeld & Nicolson Archives 160–1*

The Duke of Rutland: 19

Saltykov-Skchedrin State Public Library, Leningrad: 197 left

Scala, Milan: *34 ; Hamlyn Group Picture Library 32*

Duncan Schiedt, Indiana: 242–3

Staatliche Antikensammlung, Munich: 12

Staatsbibliothek, Berlin: 162

Stiftsbibliothek, St Gallens: 13

Dr Jaromir Svoboda, Prague: 137

Theatre-Museum, Munich: *110–1*, 189; *Weidenfeld & Nicolson Archives 136*

Universal Edition A. G. Vienna, *Weidenfeld & Nicolson Archives*: 239 above

Universal Edition, London: 240

United States Information Service, *Hamlyn Group Picture Library*: 216 left

Victoria and Albert Museum, London: 56–7, *103* above (photo John Freeman), 120, 123 above and below, 191; *Hamlyn Group Picture Library 60–1 ; Weidenfeld & Nicolson Archives 144*

Wadsworth Atheneum, Hartford, Connecticut, *Weidenfeld & Nicolson Archives :* 207

The Wallace Collection, London: *146* above and below (photos John Freeman)

Weidenfeld & Nicolson Archives: 18, 50 right, 51 above and right, 61, 63, 66, 72, 73, 81, 105, 109, 119, 208, 125, 131, 156, *158* (photo P.Marzari), 174, 179, 181, 182, 188, 190, 192, 194–5, 204, 206, 208 (photo Robert Hupka), 244 above and below

Wiener Stadt und Landesbibliothek, Vienna: 178

Hans Wild, London: 232 below right

Valerie Wilmer, London: 211, 246

Index

Page numbers in *italic* type refer to illustrations.

Albéniz, Isaac, 200
Albinoni, Tomaso, 87, 88, 91
Albrechtsberger, Johann Georg, 161
Amati, Niccolò, 84
Arcadelt, Jacques, 66
Armstrong, Louis, 213
Arne, Thomas Augustine, *144*
atonality, 224, 226
Auber, Daniel, 181
Aubert, Louis, *202*
Auric, Georges, 208

Babbit, Milton, 235
Bach, Carl Philip Emanuel, *122*, 124
Bach, Johann Sebastian, 72, 97, 105, *107*, 109, 112, 113–16, *114*, 120, 124, 193
Bakst, Léon, *207*, *210–11*
Balakirev, Mily, 198
ballet, *146*, *210–11*
Banchieri, Adriano, 66
Bartók, Béla, 217–22, *225*
Beatles, the, *222*, 245
Bechet, Sidney, 213, *220*
Bedford, David, *240*
Beecham, Sir Thomas, *232*
Beethoven, Ludwig van, 72, 79, 114, 128–9, 129, 130, 137, 139, *151*, *160*, 160–5, *161*, *162*, *163*, *164*, *172–3*, 174
Bellini, Vincenzo, 183, *183*
Benserade, Isaac de, 92
Berg, Alban, 226
Berio, Luciano, 235
Berkeley, Lennox, *233*
Berlioz, Hector, *6*, 148, 170–3,

171, *172–3*, 173, 174–5, 181–2
Bizet, Georges, 182
Borodin, Alexander, 198
Boulanger, Nadia, 204, 208, 227
Boulez, Pierre, 230, *232*, 233–4
Boyce, William, 87, *156*
Brahms, Johannes, *155*, 167, 170, 173, *176*, 177
Britten, Benjamin, 227, *228, 229*, 231
Brown, Earle, 235
Bruckner, Anton, 173, 177–8, *178*
Buxtehude, Dietrich, 108–9
Byrd, William, 56, 71

Caccini, Giulio, 75–7
Cage, John, *234*, 235, *241*
cantata, 119–21
Carter, Elliott, 213, 235
castrati, *116*, *117*, 142–4
Cavalli, Francesco, 88
Cazzati, Maurizio, 88
cello, *157*
Chabrier, Emmanuel, 205
chamber music, 157
Charpentier, Marc-Antoine, 92, 97
Chausson, Ernest, 203
Chávez, Carlos, 217
Cherubini, Luigi, 148, 170, 180
Chopin, Frederic, 192–3, *193*
cittern, *103*
clarinet, 153
Clash, the, *223*
clavichord, 33, *120*, 124
concerto, 85–6, 138
Copland, Aaron, 213, *216*, 227
Corelli, Arcangelo, *86*, 87, 88
cornett, 21, *50*, *104*, *123*
Cornysh, William, 56

Costeley, Guillaume, 58
Couperin, François, 97–100
Cowell, Henry, 235
crumhorn, *50*
cyclicism, 185–6, 203–4
cymbals, 21, *35*

Dallapiccola, Luigi, 235
Darmstadt, *126*, 231, 233
Davis, Miles, 213, *221*
Debussy, Claude-Achille, 100, *204–5*, 205–8, *206*, *207*
Delius, Frederic, *208–9*, 209
dodecaphony, 226
Donizetti, Gaetano, 182–3
Dowland, John, 59
drums, 21, *35*; *see also* tabor
Dufay, Guillaume, *40*, *41*–4
Dunstable, John, 37–41, 44, 56
Dvorak, Antonin, 178–80, *179*, 198
Dylan, Bob, *246*

electronic music, 234, *247*
Elgar, Edward, 199–200, *200–1*, 201, 209
Etruscan musicians, *34–5*

Falla, Manuel de, 200
Farinelli (Carlo Broschi), *88*, 142
Fauré, Gabriel, 163, *202*, 203, 204, *204–5*, 208
Fayrfax, Robert, 56
Festa, Costanzo, 66
figured bass, 85
flageolet, 21
Flemish composers, 52–3
flute, 21, *39*, *50*, *72*, *99*, *103*, *111*, *147*
folk music, 16, 191, 197, 217–20
Franck, César, 173, 175–7, 185, 203

French horn, *123*
Frescobaldi, Girolamo, 88, *88*

Gabrieli, Andrea, 66, 67, 68
Gabrieli, Giovanni, 67, 68, 86
Galilei, Vincenzo, 75
Galli-Bibiena family, *110–11, 141*
Gay, John, 148
Geminiani, Francesco, 87–8
Gershwin, George, 213, 216, *217*
Gesualdo, Carlo, 66
Gibbons, Orlando, *62*
Gilbert and Sullivan, 182
Ginastera, Alberto, 217
Glazunov, Alexander, 198
Glinka, Michael, 198
Gluck, Christoph Willibald, *128*, 128–9, 144–8
goliards, 16, 18
Gombert, Nicholas, 52
Gounod, Charles, 167, 170, 173, 182
Gregorian chant, 13, 21
Gregory I, Pope, 13, *13*
Grieg, Edvard, *198*, 198–9, 201, *214*
Guarneri, Giuseppe Bartolomeo, 84
Guido of Arezzo, *15*, 15–16
guitar, 21, *62–3, 84*

Halévy, Jacques Fromental, 181
handbells, *23, 39*
Handel, George Frideric, 87, *107*, 109, 113, *115*, 116–18, *117*, 144, 148
Handl, Jacob, 60, 105
harmony, 85
harp, *10*, 19, *27, 39, 40, 47, 61, 98*, *155*
harpsichord, 33, 121–2, 149–53, *157*
Hassler, Hans Leo, 60, 105
Haydn, Franz Joseph, 128–9, 129, 130, *130*, 130–3, *131, 132, 133*, 137, *147*, 148, 149, 153, 160, 163
Hindemith, Paul, 213, 227, 231
Hafhaimer, Paul, 60, *60–1*
Holst, Gustav, 209
Honneger, Arthur, 208, 227
hurdy-gurdy (organistrum), *5*, 20–1, *39*

Indy, Vincent d', 203, 203–4
instruments, instrumental music, 18–21, 33, 56–8, 60, 61, 68–71, 72, 84, 85–91, 173
Isaac, Heinrich, 52, 105
isorhythm, 28–9
Ives, Charles, 199, 201

Janacek, Leos, 198, *198*
Jannequin, Clément, 58

jazz, 213–16, *221*
Jolivet, André, 208
Jommelli, Niccolò, 144
jongleurs, 16
Joplin, Scott, *244*
Jullien, Antoine, *194–5*

keyboard music, 56, *77*, 121–4
Kodály, Zoltan, 217, *217*

La Scala, Milan, *159*
Lalo, Edouard, 203
Landi, Stefano, 88–9
Landini, Francesco, *32*, 33
Lassus, Roland de (Orlando di Lasso), 52–3, *53*, 60, 66, *102*
Le Jeune, Claude, 58
Leclair, Jean-Marie, 87
Leibowitz, René, 231
Leoncavallo, Ruggiero, 209
Léonin, 24
Lieder, 60, 148, 167
Ligeti, György, 235
Lind, Jenny, *192*
Liszt, Franz, 167, 170, *172–3*, 173, 175, *175*, 185, *187, 190*, 192–3, 193, 193–6
Lully, Jean-Baptiste, 88–9, 92, *92–5, 94–5*, 124
lur, 21
lute, 21, *38–9, 46, 48, 58–9, 61, 61, 64–5, 70, 99, 103, 146*
Luther, Martin, 60, 71, 105
Lutoslawski, Witold, 235
lyre, *12, 34–5*

MacDowell, Edward, 199, 201
Machaut, Guillaume de, 28–32
madrigal, 32, 62–6, 71
Mahler, Gustav, 177–8, 189, 209, *212*
Marenzio, Luca, 66, 80
Martenot, Maurice, *239*
Mascagni, Pietro, 209
Mass, the, 13, *58*, 71–2
Massenet, Jules, *204–5*
Mattheson, Johann, 127, 163
Méhul, Etienne-Nicolas, 180
Meistersinger, 18, *18*
Mendelssohn, Felix, 167, 173, 174, *174*, 192–3, 193
Menuhin, Yehudi, *229, 233*
Merulo, Claudio, 68
Messiaen, Olivier, 208, 230, 231, *231*
Meyerbeer, Giacomo, 180–1, *181*
Milan, Luis, 61
Milhaud, Darius, 208, 213, *216*, 227
Miller, Glenn, *242–3*
Minnesinger, 18
monochord, 19, *27, 36–7*

monody, 75–7
Monte, Philippe de, 52, 60, 66
Monteverdi, Claudio, 66, 72–5, 80, *80*, 81, *81*, 85
Morales, Cristobal, 61
motet, 24, *26*, 27, 71–2
Mouton, Jean, 52
Mozart, Wolfgang Amadeus, 127, 128–9, 129, 130, 133–9, *134*, *135, 136, 137, 138, 139*, 142, *150*, 153, 157, 163
Mudarra, Alonzo de, 61
Muris, Jean de, 28
musique concrète, 234
Mussorgsky, Modest, 198

nationalism, 189–201
neo-Classicism, 227–9
Nielsen, Carl August, 198–9
Nijinsky, Waslaw, *207*
Nono, Luigi, 230, 235

oboe, 153
Obrecht, Jacob, 52
Ockeghem, Jean d', *26*, 51
Offenbach, Jacques, *180, 181*, 182
opera, 27, 72, 77, 81, 85, 88–9, 92–7, 101, 116–18, 119, 135–7, 140–8, 180–9; *opera comique*, 148, 182
oratorio, 118, *119*, 121, *133*, 148, 173
orchestra, orchestral music, 81–4, 124–5, 129–30, 149–60
Orff, Carl, 16
organ, 10, 18–19, *19*, 33, *63, 78*, 108–9, 121, 122–3
organistrum (hurdy-gurdy), *5*, 20–1, *39*
organum, free and parallel, 21–3

Paganini, Niccolò, *172–3, 191*, 193
Palestrina, 61, 66, *66*, 66–7, 71
panpipes, 21, *50*
Parry, C. H. H., 209
Pedrell, Felipe, 200
Penderecki, Krzysztof, 235
percussion instruments, medieval, 21
Peri, Jacopo, 75–7
Pérotin, 24, 27
Perti, Giacomo, 88
pianoforte, *121*, 121–2, 124, 167
Piccini, Niccolò, 148
polyphony, 21–7
polytextuality, 27
pop music, *222, 223*, 240–7
portative organ, *1*, 19, *27, 32*, *36–7, 40, 47*
positive organ, 19, *60–1, 69*
Poulenc, Francis, 208, 227
Prés, Josquin des, 48, *51*, 51–2

Presley, Elvis, *219*, 241
programme music, 174–7
Prokofiev, Sergei, 227
Psalms, 9, 10, 11, 59, *98*
psaltery, 19, *27, 36, 39, 46, 98*
Puccini, Giacomo, 209, *212*
Purcell, Henry, 100–1, 153, 157

Rachmaninov, Serge, *197*, 198
racket, *50*
Rameau, Jean-Philippe, *96, 97*, 100
rauschpfeife, 61, 70
Ravel, Maurice, *202*, 204, 208, *215*
rebab, *38–9*
rebec, 20, *20, 39*
recitative, 77
recorder, 21, *50, 72, 104*
Reinhardt, Django, *244*
ricercar, 68
Rimsky-Korsakov, Nikolas, *196*, 198, *210–11*
Rore, Cipriano de, 52, 66, 67, 80
Rossini, Gioacchino, 170, *172–3*, 181, 182, *182*
Rousseau, Jean-Jacques, 145
Roussel, Albert, 203
Royal Festival Hall, London, *218*
Rubinstein, Anton, 198

Sachs, Hans, *18*
Saint-Saëns, Camille, 182, 203, 204, *204–5, 205*
Salieri, Antonio, 161
Saronno Cathedral, *48*
Satie, Erik, 203, 208
Scandello, Antonio, 60
Scarlatti, Alessandro, *87*, 88, 89, 116
Scarlatti, Domenico, 124
Scheidt, Samuel, 109
Schein, Johann Hermann, 109
Schenk, Johann, 161
Schönberg, Arnold, *224*, 224–6, 233
Schubert, Franz Peter, *154*, 167, *168–9*, 170, 173, *173–4*

Schumann, Robert, 116, 167, *170*, 173, 174, 192–3, *193*
Schütz, Heinrich, 52, 109–12, *112*
Scriabin, Alexander, 198
Scribe, Eugène, 180
serialization, 233, 234–5
Sermisy, Claudin de, 58, *99*
serpent, *123*
shawm, 21, *46*
Shostakovich, Dmitri, 227
Sibelius, Jean, 198–9, *199*, 201
Smetana, Bedrich, 197, *197*, 198
sonata, 68, 85–6, 89–91; sonata form, 129
songs, medieval, 16–18
Spain, 18, 24, 60–2, 200
spinet (virginals), *56–7, 57, 74–5, 103, 106*
Spohr, Louis, 173
Spontini, Gasparo, 148, 180
Stanford, Charles Villiers, 209
Stein, Gertrude, 208
Stockhausen, Karlheinz, 230, 234–5, *236–7, 238, 239*
Stradella, Alessandro, 87
Stradivari, Antonio, 84, *84, 103*
Strauss, Johann, the Younger, *176, 177*, 182
Strauss, Richard, 189, 231, *232*
Stravinsky, Igor, 198, 213, 227, 227–9, *230, 231*
string quartet, 157–60
stringed instruments, 19–21, *108*
Sweelinck, Jan Pieterszoon, 108
symphony, 89, 124–5, 129, 173–80

tabor, *17, 27, 42, 61, 72*
Tailleferre, Germaine, 208
Tallis, Thomas, 56, 71, *71*
tambourine, 21, *29, 70*
Tartini, Giuseppe, 88, *90*
Tchaikovsky, Piotr Ilitch, 178–80, *179*, 198
Telemann, George Philipp, 87, *87*
Tinctoris, Johannes, 49
tone rows, 224, 233

Torelli, Giuseppe, 87, 88
Toscanini, Arturo, *208*
tromba marina, *46*
trombone, *50, 70, 70*, 71
troubadours, *trouvères*, 16–18
trumpets, 21, *22, 28, 46, 47, 60, 98, 104*
twelve-tone composition, *see* dodecaphony

Valentino, Nicolò, 67
Varèse, Edgar, 235
Vaughan Williams, Ralph, 209, *213*
Verdelot, Philippe, 66
Verdi, Giuseppe, *158*, 170, 183–5, *184*
Véron, Louis, 180
vièle (fiddle), 20, *36–7, 39, 47*
Vienna, *124–5, 125, 136, 161*
Villa-Lobos, Heitor, 213, 217
viola da gamba, *58–9, 106, 111*
violin, *48, 61, 70*, 84, 91, 92, *93, 103, 108*
viols, 20, 33, *48, 57, 61, 70, 103, 109*
Vitry, Philippe de, 27, 28
Vivaldi, Antonio, 88, *89*, 91, *91*, 138–9

Wagner, Richard, 18, 181, 185, *185, 186, 186–9, 187, 188, 188–9*, 226
Walton, William, 209
Weber, Carl Maria von, 185, *185*
Webern, Anton von, 226, *226*
Wert, Giaches de, 66
Wesley, Samuel Sebastian, 173
Willaert, Adrian, 49, *50*, 52, 66, 67, 68, 80
Williams, Ralph Vaughan, *see* Vaughan Williams
wind instruments, 21, *105*, 153
Wolf, Hugo, 167, *171*, 189

Xenakis, Iannis, 230

Zarlino, Gioseffo, 67